Wawne Fer

By Martin L

First Published in July 2003
Reprinted with additional material in September 2003
This expanded edition contains additions and amendments
to the original text together with more images and was first
published in April 2015
Copyright: Martin Limon, 2003, 2015, 2018
Published by Popinjay Press

The sources used in writing this book are shown as ( ) in the text and are explained in the footnotes at the end.

Image above: black and white photograph of around 1900 showing a keel passing in front of Wawne Ferry.

Image below: The Holderness Hunt crossing the River Hull c. 1900

Contents:
Preface
Chapter One: Beginnings
Chapter Two: Changes
Chapter Three: Within Living Memory
Chapter Four: Demise
Postscript

Preface

I moved to Thearne in 1987 at a time when the only visible reminders of Wawne Ferry were the existence of the street names "Ferry Lane" on the Woodmansey side of the river, "Ferry Road" on the Wawne side and a public house in Wawne Road, Bransholme called "The Wawne Ferry". In the late 1960's the County Council had warned the unwary traveller that "Wawne Ferry was closed permanently" by means of a large sign on the main Hull to Beverley road but by the late 1980's even this sign had disappeared. Yet, the number of cyclists, usually foreign visitors, who halted in Thearne, on the way to the River Hull, and asked for directions to the ferry, surprised me. This was over 40 years after the ferry had closed for the last time! By 2015 little had changed and the roads on both sides of the River Hull leading to the site of Wawne Ferry remain narrow and peaceful cul-de-sacs untroubled by the heavy traffic of modern times. Those arriving at the river on the Thearne side (near Prospect Farm) will still see some of the cobblestones of the ferry landing (now largely hidden under the riverbank.)

In writing this history I am indebted to the many local people who have shared their memories of the time when the ferry was in operation or provided information from their own studies:

Mr A. Mann,
Mr L. Ransom
Mrs A. Hinch
Mr M. Jackson
Ms M. Botham,
Mr J. Beaulah
Mr B. Newlove
Mr L Heathcote
Mr B. Wardill
Mr C. Nicklas
Mrs N. Train
Mrs A. Pearson

Mrs J. Tasker
Mrs B. Cawood
Mrs M. Walker
Mrs J. Gibbins
Mr T. Hincks
Mr J. Lawson
Mr J. Robinson
Mrs M. Rodmell
Mrs A. Loss
Mr M. Yates
Mr R. Nicholson
Mr J. Nicholson
Mr F. Norton
Mr and Mrs A. Hood
Mrs J. Davies
Mr Rob Haywood

Thanks also go to the staff of the following for their help in researching the history of the ferry:
East Riding of Yorkshire Council County Archives Service, Beverley
Hull City Archives, Hull
Beverley Local Studies Library
Hull Local History Library
Sutton Museum
University of Hull Archive
The Bass Museum

It is fortunate that numerous photographers chose to capture images of the ferry from the late nineteenth century onwards. I would like to thank those people who lent copies of these.

In producing this 2015 edition I would like to thank Les Fisher, Penny Stewart and Peter Croton for their help.

Martin Limon, Thearne, June 2003 and March 2015

Abbreviations:

VCH: Victoria County History

PRO: Public Record Office (Kew)

ERCA: East Riding of Yorkshire County Archive Service

HCCA: Hull City Archive

Chapter One: Beginnings

In an age of super-ferries plying their trade across the seas of the world it is, perhaps, easy to forget the more humble origins of ferries as a means of crossing rivers and estuaries for the conveyance of people and goods. In 1948 the Ministry of Transport published a report on river ferries operating in the United Kingdom and found that there were still forty-four vehicular river ferries providing a service.(1) In the nineteenth century, before a rapid expansion of bridge building, there were even more ferryboats operating. Locally, Spencer's Drainage Map of 1848 shows fifteen shuttle services across the River Hull, including ferries at Grovehill (Beverley), Weel, Wawne and Stoneferry. At Wawne, in addition to the ferry, there was Hudson's Shuttle at Gibraltar Farm and Ramsay's Shuttle (both in the south-western corner of the township) (2)

In an age before bridges or when bridges were few in number river ferries provided a vital link in road communications. On the River Hull a ferry at Drypool existed by 1273, crossing from the land of the lords of Sutton on the east to the land of Gilbert de Aton. Further upstream at Stoneferry, the probable site of a stone paved ford, there was a ferry by the mid 14th century. (3) On the lower part of the River Hull the first bridge (North Bridge) was built in 1541 to give better communications with the fortifications being built on the eastern bank of the river. (4) Upstream from Hull the nearest bridge linked Beverley with Holderness (near present day Tickton). A bridge there is first mentioned in c.1260, the year it was destroyed by rebels who were trying to isolate Holderness. It seems to have been rebuilt by 1279.n (5)

Image above: Hull Bridge (near Tickton) in the 19th century. Wawne Ferry provided a useful way to cross the River Hull for travellers between Beverley and Wawne / Sutton because the distance by road via Hull Bridge, Routh and Meaux to Wawne was about six miles.

Although older than either Stoneferry or Drypool ferries, the precise origins of Wawne (or Waghen) Ferry are not recorded. It seems to have been a link in an "ancient highway". This extended eastwards from Brough (the Roman town of Petuaria) to Rowley and thence to the River Hull. Crossing the river at the site of the later Wawne Ferry this highway followed a route to south–eastern Holderness. (6) The crossing point of the River Hull was a place where the river was occasionally shallow enough to be forded. (7) To assist travellers a layer of stones was laid on the riverbed from bank to bank. In 1721 these stones were removed because of their interference with the flow of the River Hull although some remains were still there in 1852. A report of the time said "the bottom of the river is exceedingly irregular and at Wawne Ferry there is a sudden rise of about five feet being the remains of an ancient ford composed of hard material." (8) On the western side of the river part of this highway comprised the modern-day Ferry Lane and Long Lane (9), while on the eastern side it occupied a strip of higher land linking present-day Wawne, Sutton and Bilton. (10)

This shallow point on the River Hull at the site of an existing ford was a natural choice for a ferry service. Whether the ferry came into existence before or after the Norman Conquest (1066) is unknown. The earliest written references to it call the ferry "et passagium" (11) - the passage over the River Hull. As late as 1928 the ferry was described as the Beverley-Sutton ferry. (12) However it is impossible to give a precise date to when the ferry service began. We do know that the ferry was in existence before 1136 when William le Gros, Earl of Albemarle, gave lands at Wawne, or its alternative name of Waghen, to the Cistercian Abbey of Meaux together with "a free passage over the River Hull". It is probable that he held these lands and the ferry rights as a tenant of the Archbishop of York.

The beginnings of the Cistercian order, which aimed to lead a more simple and devout religious life, can be traced back to eleventh century France. As the movement spread they built a number of great monasteries and a network of daughter houses including Fountains Abbey (founded in 1132). It was from here that a monk called Adam and twelve others set out to establish a Cistercian monastery at Meaux on lands donated by William Le Gros, Lord of Holderness, as a penance for failing to go on a pilgrimage to the Holy Land.

In 1150 Henry Murdoc, the Archbishop, confirmed the grant of "the passage of the River Hull at Waghen" to the Abbey of Meaux reserving to himself various rents payable to him "at his manor at Beverley." (13) These rents contributed the fairly large sum of £3 or £4 to the value of the manor of Beverley in the 14th and 16th centuries. (14) The archbishop's manor house where the ferry rent was paid was at Hall Garth from where the present-day Long Lane led south and then east to Thearne. (15) These rents continued to be payable into the twentieth century when they amounted to £7.13s.0d (£7.65) each year. In 1154 King Stephen confirmed the foundation of Meaux and the "passage of the River Hull at Waghen" with two carucates of land. However it seems that the ferry may have been the subject of a dispute between Archbishop Roger and the Abbey for it was "again resumed by that prelate" until recovered by the abbey in the time of Alexander the 4th abbot (c 1197). (16)

For the first 400 years of its 800 year recorded history the rights to Wawne Ferry belonged to the monks of Meaux Abbey. During the administration of Philip the second abbot of Meaux (1160-1182) the abbey acquired lands at Brantingham and Brough. These lands contained a stone quarry and it was from this stone that "the permanent buildings of the monastery were afterwards constructed." (17) The stone was shipped from the Humber to Wawne Ferry and from there it was transported to Meaux.

By the mid thirteenth century the monastic community included sixty monks and ninety lay brothers – the manual workers, usually illiterate, who assisted in building projects and in the work on the granges (farms) sometimes at some distance from the Abbey itself. (18) Perhaps it was these lay brothers who operated the ferryboat that made the short crossing from the Thearne side of the River Hull to the Wawne side

What of the communities served by the ferry in the middle ages? The first significant settlement around Beverley was the monastery of *Inderauuda* founded by St John of Beverley around 705 AD. After his death in 721 he was buried at the monastery and subsequently canonised (1037). The reported miracles occurring at his tomb meant an influx of pilgrims looking for cures or to worship. (19) A trading settlement grew around the monastery especially in the years following the Norman Conquest. (20)

Until the rise of Hull from the end of the 13th century Beverley's position as the trading centre of the region was pre-eminent. The growth of Beverley was encouraged by the Archbishop of York; he secured royal charters for markets and fairs. From the early 12th century there was a weekly market in Beverley and fairs three times a year. Both served to bring in buyers and sellers from a large area of North East England.

In addition Beverley established itself as a centre for wool processing and cloth making during the 12th century and by 1390 a total of thirty eight trades (including weaving, fulling and dyeing) are in evidence in the town. The growth of commerce was helped when in the 12th century the Archbishop of York (as Lord of the Manor of Beverley) persuaded the people to make a channel from the River Hull of sufficient depth to carry ships. With the arrival of the Flemings in the town (as craftsmen or wool merchants) from the 12th century a further boost was given to the town's economic growth. Raw wool was exported to the cloth towns of the Low Countries (like Bruges) and the Flemish merchants active in Beverley gave their name to Flammengaria, later Flemingate. Similarly in the 13th century Meaux Abbey was taking part in the wool trade on a large scale.

Meaux in 1280 had 11,000 sheep, mostly in Holderness, the richest grazing land in the north of England. (21) In these circumstances of growing economic prosperity the value of the ferry at Wawne linking wool production with wool processing is obvious. Later documents refer to " a ferry over the River Hull from Wawne to the parish of Thearne *"or of whatever extent that ferry might be."* (22) This might imply that the ferry operated from Wawne to places other than Thearne although whether this meant Beverley is not recorded. However, given the fact that in neither Thearne nor Woodmansey does the ground anywhere reach over 7 metres and that the road leading to the ferry was frequently flooded it seems possible that the ferryboat did ply further afield.

Although a ferry was not mentioned in the Domesday Book Wawne itself was. William the Conquerors great survey of all England, undertaken in 1086, records that "eleven villagers and two smallholders have three ploughs." (23) In 1086 Wawne belonged partly to the Archbishop of York and partly to Drogo de Bevere, Lord of Holderness. Since Holderness lacked natural building stone the flimsy dwellings of Wawne were built of mud or turf. Archaeological discoveries in Hull have revealed the same kind of dwellings at the early village of Wyke where the River Hull met the River Humber. Dr Barbara English, lecturer in medieval history at the University of Hull, said "they lived in thatched houses built of mud which most shared with whatever animals they owned. Flooding was a constant danger. Some might have a timber frame but most would be mud with a thatched roof made from peat, reeds and turf." (24) The marshes of the Hull Valley provided many *turbaries* or turf cutting areas and the villagers seem to have used turfs for "building their houses, roofing them and for fuel." (25)

Some turfs were sent further afield for in the 13th century a burgess of Beverley negotiated 22 cartloads of turf from Wawne each year. The establishment of Meaux Abbey (by 1150) stimulated the local economy for by 1160 "the monks employed nearly 200 tenants there, all paying rent, and providing the abbey with corn and hay, bread and beer, geese and hens." (26) Although we lack specific evidence about the use of Wawne Ferry at this time, Abbey farms in the Wawne and Sutton area probably used the link to supply the growing market town of Beverley. Pilgrims from Holderness visiting the shrine of St John of Beverley were another likely source of income for the ferry. Although we know nothing of those who operated the ferry on behalf of Meaux Abbey (either directly or as tenants) it seems likely that they too would have lived in a crude mud-built house near the ferry-crossing and supporting themselves by farming. In 1377-1388 the ferry was valued at 60 shillings. (27)

Conditions would have been little different across the river in Thearne, This tiny hamlet with a name derived from 'thorn tree' lay about a quarter of a mile from the ferry but the low-lying nature of the land meant that the road leading to it was frequently flooded. Thearne was one of the 'water towns' of Beverley and belonged to the Archbishop of York. It was situated on a patch of boulder clay that helped to raise the village above the level of the waterlogged carrs close by. In days gone by there was a saying that Thearne "was fit for nothing but frogs and toads." (28)

After 1378 there was a chantry chapel at Thearne where a priest said prayers for the spiritual benefit of the deceased. It is therefore possible that Wawne Ferry was used by people east of the river to reach the chapel until this was suppressed in 1548 during the reign of Henry the Eighth. Few people lived in Thearne itself; there were only 87 poll tax payers for Thearne and Woodmansey combined in 1377. (29)

To understand the location and importance of Sutton-on-Hull in the days before Hull even existed it is necessary to look at the topography of the area. The village stood on a ridge of higher ground stretching from Wawne (or Waghen) to Bilton. The ridge was surrounded by water and marshland and despite the activities of the monks in draining these marshes by cutting channels (like the Fore-Dike) or enlarging existing streams and ditches, much of the low-lying land remained waterlogged. The cultivated land lay along the ridge of dry land on which the village stood. (30) In 1086 the recorded population of Sutton was eighteen (probably the number of households). In 1377, 299 adults paid the poll tax. (31) Meaux Abbey acquired a large estate in Sutton from the 12th century onward including meadow land and pasturage rights which together were worth £16 a year. (32) The better quality meadows for cattle, oxen and sheep lay north of the ridge. In addition the drainage dikes and pools in Sutton provided fishing for the lords of the manor and other landowners.

The place name was probably derived from the Anglo-Saxon settlers of England from the 5th century onwards and may mean 'south farm'. Mentioned in the Domesday Book of 1086 as Sudtone there was a chapel here occupying the site of the later church although the dead of the village had to be taken to Wawne for burial. It was not until the fourteenth century that the lord of the manor, Sir John de Sutton, decided to replace the chapel with something grander. St James's Church was built using locally made bricks and stone brought up-river to Stoneferry and then by the Antholme Dyke to Sutton. The church was dedicated in the year 1349, the year of the Black Death, and this great pestilence seems to have delayed further work on the building. The west end and the brick tower were not added until the beginning of the fifteenth century and were built in the 'Perpendicular Style' then fashionable.

Often referred to as Sutton-in-Holderness the village was one of the largest in East Yorkshire and in 1377 as many as two hundred and ninety nine adults paid the poll tax. Life here, as elsewhere, was dominated by farming with the cultivated land being on the ridge where the village stood and beyond these arable fields were the marshes and carrs that, when drained, became commons and meadows. An act of Parliament enclosed the open fields of Sutton in 1763 and in a directory of 1823 eighteen farmers were named along with the usual trades and occupations of self-reliant communities of the time. It seems likely that Wawne Ferry was, in medieval times, an important link in an old road system going from Beverley to Wawne, Sutton-on-Hull, Bilton, Preston, Hedon and other villages in Holderness.

Image above: Church Street Sutton around 1931

Image above: A statue by the artist Chris Womald created in 2010 to commemorate Beverley's medieval crafts and guilds. It stands at the head of Beverley Beck: the channel linking the town with the River Hull and used by Flemish and Beverley merchants to export raw wool and cloth to Europe.

Chapter 2: Changes

The first major change to affect the ferry was the dissolution of the monasteries during the reign of Henry VIII. The monasteries owned and exploited vast acres and by the fifteenth century the monks and canons owned something like a quarter of the land of England. When Thomas Cromwell, Lord Chancellor, put into Henry's head the idea of disciplining those who would dispute the King's new authority over the Church of England while filling a depleted treasury, the monasteries were vulnerable. The process began with the smaller institutions where " manifest sin, vicious, carnal and abominable living is daily used." The Suppression Act of 1536 transferred all the lands, buildings and possessions of these smaller abbeys to the crown. The fate of the larger abbeys, of which Meaux Abbey was one, was not long delayed. In 1539, following the rebellion of the Pilgrimage of Grace, Henry turned his attention to demolition of the larger monasteries.

When the commissioners of Henry VIII visited Meaux Abbey the community consisted of the abbot and 24 monks. Their gross yearly income was described as about £445. (33) In 1540 the Abbot of Meaux, Richard Stopes (or his successor Richard Draper), surrendered his lands and possessions (including the ferry at Waghen) to the king. (34) It is unclear what effect, if any, this transfer of ownership had on the fortunes of the ferry for there is a lack of evidence. Probably of more critical importance were the economic fortunes of the places the ferry served. By the 1530s Beverley had "declined a long way from its peak in the 13th and 14th centuries." (35) Visitors of the time commented on the decay of its houses and tenements and the decline of cloth making in Beverley following the rise of other centres of the industry in the West Riding. By the end of the 17th century it seems that the population of the town had fallen from "5000 in the Middle Ages to about 3000." (36) Beverley remained a market town but was no longer a manufacturing centre.

In 1584 the Crown leased the river crossing, the boats and tolls to Lancelot Alford. (37) The financial problems of Charles I led to the grant of manorial properties in Wawne (including the ferry) to the Corporation of the City of London in return for loans (September 1629). The name Wawne is derived from 'quagmire' and the continuing drainage problems of the area are well illustrated by a survey of these lands in 1650 that reported that of the 3,888 acres held about 1,800 acres were "oppressed with water." (38) In August 1651 these same properties were conveyed by lease to Sir Joseph Ashe bringing about the long association of the ferry with the Ashe / Windham family which was to last until 1911. Sir Joseph Ashe was a major innovator in land drainage and took steps to divert water into drains connected with the Forth Dike. He also raised the riverbanks to prevent water getting onto his Wawne lands. In Wawne Carrs he cut a new drain and built two windmills to lift the water from it into the River Hull. All these improvements served to make the land around Wawne more productive beyond the usual fishing and wildfowling. (39)

Sir Joseph Ashe's eldest daughter Katherine (1652-1729) married William Windham of Felbrigg Hall Norfollk in 1669. A marriage between Katherine's son Joseph and her niece Martha eventually brought *ownership* of Wawne Manor into the Windham family. In 1734 this comprised among other things over 4000 acres of land and "a passage over the River Hull in Waghen and Sutton." (40)

Of the day-to-day operation of the ferry in the 17th and early 18th century we know little. However its usefulness as a link between the east and west banks of the River Hull is perhaps illustrated best by the story of the attempted flight of Sir John Hotham from Hull during the English Civil War. Hotham's early defiance of King Charles I in 1642 is well known. As Governor of Hull Hotham had denied Charles entry into the town in April 1642 but as the war progressed his loyalty to

Parliament wavered. His disloyalty was soon apparent and preparations were in hand by June 1643 to forestall any plans he might have to deliver up the town to the king. (41) On June 29th 1643 forces loyal to the parliamentary cause effectively seized control of the town. Forewarned of this Hotham made his escape from Hull via Beverley Gate and rode north on a borrowed horse with the aim of reaching his fortified house at Scorborough, nine miles to the north. In order to reach this he had no need to cross the River Hull and yet chose to do so, perhaps in an attempt to evade pursuers. He therefore left the Beverley Road and turned down to Stoneferry, intending to cross the River Hull into Holderness. However arriving there and "not meeting with a boat, and the river being too rapid to swim over" (42), Hotham moved on to Wawne Ferry where he faced the same problem. According to Oliver, the 19th century Beverley historian, " the ferry boat had proceeded up the river with a party of pleasure and he was once more disappointed in his hope of crossing the water." (43) Delayed by these misguided attempts to cross the River Hull news of his escape had by then reached the parliamentary forces occupying Beverley. As Hotham attempted to pass through the town he was recognised and arrested by the parliamentary commander, Colonel Boynton. Imprisoned with his son on board the ship *Hercules* moored in the Humber both were closely guarded until the ship set sail for London. On the 15th of July 1643 they were sent to the Tower to await trial and execution on a charge of high treason to the Commonwealth.

      The eighteenth century saw changes in communications that must have impacted on the use of the ferry as well as changes at the ferry itself. Those arriving at the west side of the River Hull travelled either by Ferry Lane or Thearne Lane (formerly called Thearne Road and Old Wife Carr Road) to the Hull-Beverley highway. This major artery grew in importance as Hull developed as a thriving port from the Middle Ages. The need to keep the road 'dry is indicated by the writings of the traveller Celia Fienes who said in 1697:

"We went from Beverley to Hull six miles all upon a causeway secured with two little rivers running on each side."

As traffic grew in the eighteenth century the importance of keeping the western approaches to the ferry in good repair is indicated by documents in the East Riding Archive. Under the Highways Act of 1555 the parishioners of Thearne, like those elsewhere, were made responsible for the maintenance of roads. They had to elect a Surveyor of Highways annually and under his direction spend six days a year of unpaid labour repairing the roads. This system of 'statute labour' was particularly difficult at a place like Thearne where the low-lying nature of the land meant that the roads were often flooded. Under the 1555 act local Justices of the Peace were told to inspect the roads and the courts could punish parishes that neglected their duties. In 1717 the inhabitants of Thearne, Woodmansey and Beverley Parks were indicted for the "non-repair of the highway from Newbridge to Waghen Ferry." (44) In 1736 another indictment was issued against the inhabitants of Thearne for the "non-repair of the highway from the west side of Waghen alias Waun ferry over Thearne Carr onto Hull Road adjoining Wharton Bridge." (45)

Soon there were new developments in road communication as Hull and Beverley became the focal points of several turnpike roads. The earliest turnpike was that of 1744 affecting the road from Hull to Beverley. The idea behind a turnpike trust was that they would take over a road, improve it but charge travellers a toll for using it. At 'Toll Bar Cottage' in Woodmansey (the junction of Long Lane and Ferry Lane) a toll-keeper collected money from those joining the road here including those who arrived from Wawne Ferry. The tolls varied according to the type of vehicle or traffic using it with a coach or wagon drawn by four horses paying one shilling (5p) and someone on horseback one and a half old pence (less than 1p). However one of the complaints of travellers joining the main road at Woodmansey (or Thearne) Bar was that they still had to pay the full toll for a limited use of the road.

In 1767 came a turnpike scheme that, if it had been implemented, would have replaced Wawne Ferry with a bridge. The new turnpike road was to start at Woodmansey Bar and go via Ferry Lane Thearne to a new bridge over the River Hull at Wawne. It would then go to the White Cross - Beverley turnpike via Meaux and the Hedon- Patrington turnpike via Sutton. It was proposed that the new bridge at Wawne Ferry would be paid for out of the County rates "as other bridges are and have been". (46) Another document from 1767 in the East Riding Archive is the " Account of Robert Appleton, clerk of the peace," relating to the proposed bridge at Wawne Ferry." Appleton made an expenses claim for £1 15s 0d (£1.75 in modern money) for "writing a long letter to Sir Robert Hildyard" and thirteen other justices acquainting them that the East Riding JPs had "received two petitions at the last sessions requesting them to build a bridge over the River Hull." (47)

The scheme, already approved at a public meeting, was to be put to Parliament but, in the event, it came to nothing. In part this was due to the opposition of Beverley Corporation who believed that such a scheme might be prejudicial to the town's interest. (48) Five years later a modified scheme was suggested with an alternative bridge at Stoneferry. As one of its supporters, Charles Pool of Hull, pointed out:

"The former scheme by way of Wawne Ferry may at first appear preferable to this by Stoneferry as it would be a mile nearer from Beverley to Hedon but when it is considered that the whole road from Thearne Barr to the river is very bad, this plan is surely more eligible." (49) This scheme too came to nothing. Objections from Beverley Corporation who had always jealously guarded their navigational rights on the River Hull thwarted these plans. Stoneferry had to wait until 1905 until it saw a bridge.

   The abortive bridge scheme of 1767 may have given an impetus to improvements at the Wawne side of the river. In the centuries since the ferry had begun there must have been some form of accommodation for the generations of ferrymen who worked the service since they needed to be at hand when needed. Presumably the ferryman's house would have been built of mud in much the same way as other dwellings in Wawne in the Middle Ages and later. These flimsy dwellings would have been constantly rebuilt on the same site. By the eighteenth century brick was more readily available and in June 1776 we are told that a Mr Lyth was being paid 1s 6d a day (about 8p in today's money) for nine day's work at Wawne Ferry. (50) At the same time one of the regular workers on the Windham estate, George Stephenson, was being paid 4d a day for "handing brick to the bricklayers." The work in hand was probably the new Wawne Passage House (later the Anchor Inn /Windham Arms). One of its first occupants may have been "John Kerby of Waughen Ferry" who was named in a document of 1777. (51) Other recorded tenants of the new house were a Mr Judson and a Mr Clough who apparently took possession in January 1783. (52) The nearby Bamforth Farmhouse on the south side of Ferry Road dates from the same period. (53) There were other additions to the Wawne Passage House in the mid-Victorian era: stables and outbuildings connected with the thirty-three acre farm that went with the tenancy. (54)

Image above: Ferry Lane Thearne in 2015

Further entries in the Wawne account book reveal expenditure on gravel and paving at the ferry when a new dock was made. (55) The tidal River Hull often left a morass of mud and other debris and this meant a constant battle to keep the dock clean. In August 1781 George Stephenson (and a certain Mr Richardson) were paid 8s 0d for "cleaning out the ferry dock" (56)

It has been said that the average life of a wooden boat in either the eighteenth or nineteenth century was about twenty-six years and so there must have been a constant need to keep the ferryboat in a good state of repair. The boat in use at Wawne in the late 1770s seems to have been near the end of its useful life for in 1778 and in 1779 considerable sums were spent in repairing it.(57) The work was carried out by William Wiseman, a shipbuilder of Lime Street in Hull. (58) It seems, however, that his efforts and the money spent were in vain for early in 1780 the ferryboat sank. On January 26th 1780 we are told that twelve shillings was paid "for raising the ferry boat from the bottom of the river." (59) Despite the sinking Mr Wiseman did not forfeit the confidence of the Windhams (or perhaps their steward, Stephen Hawke) (60). Wiseman was asked to build a new ferryboat and was paid £60 for the work. (61) Further sums were paid out on iron work for the new boat. The first launching of the new ferry in July 1780 was the cause of some celebration for we are told that eight shillings was spent on ale that day and a further four shillings and six pence on ale in November 1780 when "taking the old ferry boat to pieces." (62)

At the beginning of the 19th century the combined roles of ferryman, farmer and publican were well established and we have more evidence from trade directories, census returns and newspaper accounts about those who lived and worked from "Ferry House" as it was now known. A directory of 1823 shows that William Breeding (born 1777) was the victualler of the Anchor Inn (63) and he would have made part of his living from sales of food and drink to those using the ferry and those involved in the thriving trade on the River Hull. Among the list of licenses granted by JPs to publicans in 1826 was "Wiiliam Breeding of the Anchor at Wawne". (64) The public house was still called the Anchor on the Ordnance Survey map of 1853.

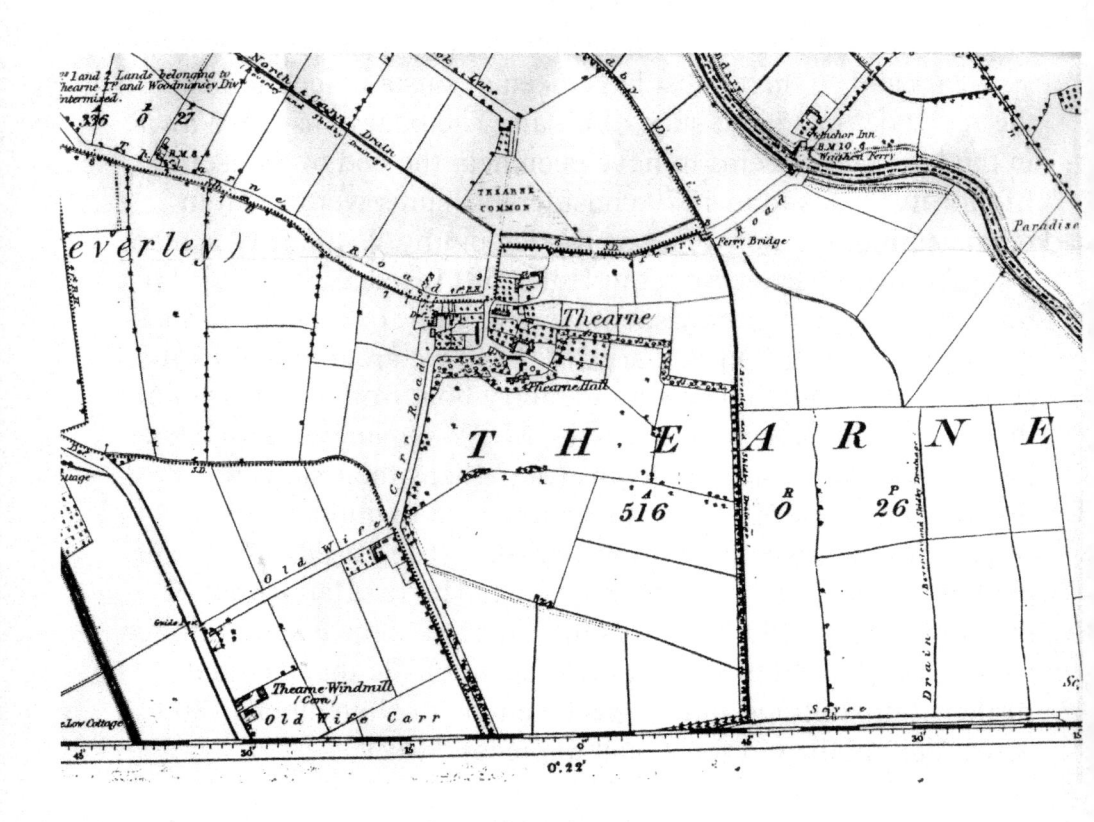

Image above: 1853 Ordnance Survey Map

As the map shows, travellers from Beverley wishing to use Wawne Ferry could use either of two routes from the main Hull to Beverley Road: Ferry Lane or Thearne Lane (on this map marked as Old Wife Carr Road)

The 1851 census return for Wawne shows that William Breeding was a seventy-four year old widower with a forty-five year old son (also called William) and a thirty-five year old unmarried daughter (Mary). In the 1851 census William Junior was described as a farm labourer and Mary as a house servant. In 1851 three other boys aged 15,14 and 9 were also living at the Anchor Inn. (65) No doubt with a ferry, an inn and a thirty-three acre farm to run William Breedin Senior needed all his family's help.

William Breeding Junior (1806-1878) continued to operate the ferry, the farm and the Anchor Inn after his father's death. The 1861 census describes him as an unmarried publican and farmer of Wawne living with his sisters. A year later a report in the Beverley Guardian newspaper recorded:

"Wawne Hospitality – On Friday the 6th instant, John Ramsey Esquire of Beverley, through respect to his labourers who worked for him during the time he occupied the Ings Farm, gave them a substantial dinner of roast beef and plum pudding and a good supply of barley beer and grog, at Mr W. Breeding's Anchor Inn, Wawne Ferry. The usual toasts on such occasions were given, and the health of Mr Ramsey was drunk with musical honours. The same gentleman gave an excellent tea a few weeks ago to several old women, at the Anchor Inn." (66)

William Breeding Junior died in 1878 and left money to his unmarried sister Elizabeth Breeding (born 1809). (67)

Between 1879 and 1950 the fortunes of the public house and Wawne Ferry were in the hands of the Brewer family or their relatives. By 1879 the landlord of the Anchor Inn and ferryman, was James Brewer, born in Little Weighton in 1836. In the 1881 census James Brewer is recorded as being forty-five years old and a farmer of 33 acres. His wife Rebecca Richardson (born in Routh) was forty-two. The Brewers had nine sons and three daughters the eldest being Joseph aged 22 and the youngest, Robert Brewer, an infant of 6 months. Ten of the children had been born in the hamlet of Arnold (near Long Riston) between the years 1859 and 1877. (68) When James Brewer died in 1889 Rebecca continued to live at the Anchor Inn and a year later married William Dunning Gray (1837-1919). (69) Bulmer's Directory of 1892 shows that Gray was now the victualler of the Anchor Inn and the ferryman. By 1901 Rebecca had left and the tenancy of the ferry, farm and the public house had been taken over by her daughter Alice (born 1860) and her son-in-law John Wood (born 1853). (70) The seventh of Rebecca's children, Donald Brewer (1870-1960) was himself to become the tenant of the farm, ferryman and innkeeper. He was to continue in these roles and still worked as a ferryman when well into his seventies. Donald Brewer had been born in Arnold and at the time of the 1891 census he was living and working at Jackson's Farm Wawne. In 1907 he married Sarah Spear of Skirlaugh and was the licensee of the Windham Arms from at least August of that year.

The 1881 census record for Ferry House Wawne

Name	Relation to Head of Family	Married / Unmarried	Age last birthday	Occupation	Where born
James Brewer	Head of Family	married	45	Farmer of 33 acres employing three boys	Little Weighton
Rebecca Brewer	wife	married	42	Farmers Wife	Routh
Joseph Brewer	son	unmarried	22	Farm Labourer	Arnold
Alice Brewer	daughter	unmarried	20		Arnold
Edward Brewer	son	unmarried	18	Farm Labourer	Arnold
Ellen Brewer	daughter	unmarried	16		Arnold
George Brewer	son	unmarried	14	Farm Labourer	Arnold
Frank Brewer	son	unmarried	12	Farm Labourer	Arnold
Donald Brewer	son	unmarried	10	Scholar	Arnold
Katherine Brewer	daughter	unmarried	8	Scholar	Arnold
James Brewer	son	unmarried	6	Scholar	Arnold
Thomas Brewer	son	unmarried	4	Scholar	Arnold
Walter	son	Unmarri	2		Wawne

Brewer		ed			
Robert Brewer	son	unmarried	6 months		Wawne

1891 census record for the Anchor Inn, Wawne

Name	Relation to Head of Family	Married/ Unmarried	Age last birthday	Occupation	Where born
William D Gray	Head of family	married	54	Farmer and publican	Dunswell, Yorkshire
Rebecca Gray	wife	married	52		Routh, Yorkshire
Kate Brewer	step daughter	single	19	General servant domestic	Arnold
James Brewer	step son	single	16	Farm servant	Arnold
Tom Brewer	step son	single	14	scholar	Arnold
Robert Brewer	step son	single	10	scholar	Wawne
Walter Brewer	step son	married	11	scholar	Wawne

Emma Brewer	step daughter	single	7	scholar	Wawne
William Willey	servant	single	20	Farm servant	Wawne
Ellen Walker	step daughter	married	26		Arnold

| Edward Walker | Step grandson | single | 7 | scholar | Whitedale, Yorkshire |

1901 census record for the Windham Arms Public House, Wawne

Name	Relation to Head of Family	Married / Unmarried	Age last Birthday	Occupation	Where born
John Wood	Head of family	married	47	Innkeeper and farmer	Wawne
Alice Wood	wife	married	40	pub	Arnold
James B Wood	son		13		Hull
Francis Wood	son		12		Hull
John Wood	son		7		Wawne
Richard Wood	son		3		Wawne
Frederick Wilkinson	servant	single	17	Carter on farm	Hessle
Mary Thompson	servant	single	14	General servant domestic	Cottingham

1911 Census Record for the Windham Arms, Wawne

Name	Relation to	Particulars as to	Age last	Occupation	Where born

	Head of Family	marriage	Birthday		
Donald Brewer	head	Married for for 4 years	41	Ferry, farm, publican	Skirlaugh
Mrs D Brewer	wife	Married for 4 years	46	Public house work	Skirlaugh
James Hardy		single	50	Farm labourer	Frodingham
Elsie Mariah Gibbons		single	14	Domestic servant	Beverley
John Henry Barrow		single	14	Ferry and Farm Servant	Beverley

Image above: Donald Brewer c. 1911

It was in August 1907 that he found himself in trouble with the law. He appeared in a magistrate's court with his solicitor Harry Wray to answer the charge that he had allowed drunkenness on his premises. Two labourers, Charles Milner and J. Raines were also in court for being drunk.

The Hull Daily Mail of August 17th 1907 described what happened:

" P.C. Bell visited the Windham Arms, Wawne, to take a sample under the Food and Drugs Act. In the kitchen he saw Milner and Raines each with a glass in front of them. They were both drunk. Raines seemed to be asleep and was reeling from side to side in his chair. Mr and Mrs Brewer passed in and out of the kitchen and could see the condition the men were in."
In mitigation Harry Wray pleaded that his client did not know that the men were on his premises at all as his maidservant had served them in his absence. However the magistrates were not inclined to accept his excuses and fined Donald Brewer seven shillings plus costs while Milner and Raines each had to pay a fine of two shillings and sixpence plus costs.

During the tenancy of James Brewer the Windhams had became involved in an acrimonious dispute with the Beverley and Barmston Drainage Commissioners. In 1880 the Commissioners had put forward a parliamentary bill for the dredging of the river Hull. A parliamentary committee that examined the bill in detail heard evidence from the land agent Henry Parker that of the obstructions in the river the worst one was at Wawne Ferry. Dredging took place in 1884 and letters of the time suggested the removal of "the Wawne Ferry ridge in view of the difficulties you say you have experienced in getting your launches over it." (71) Following the dredging of the river next to the Windham estate William George Windham became involved in litigation against the Beverley and Barmston Drainage Commissioners complaining of the damage that had been done to the river banks and trespass by the firm carrying out the dredging.

PLAN REFERRED TO IN THE PLAINTIFFS STATMENT OF CLAIM
SHOWING SLIPS IN THE BANK OF THE RIVER HULL
IN LAND OF W.G WINDHAM ESQ^{RE}
AT WAWNE
AND WHICH SLIPS REQUIRE TO BE PILED AND CHALKED AS SHOWN
ALSO SHOWING LAND DEPRECIATED
IN VALUE IN CONSEQUENCE OF
DREDGING OPERATIONS AND FOR WHICH COMPENSATION
IS CLAIMED

Scale 200 feet to the inch

Images from East Riding Archives Service DCBB/5/21

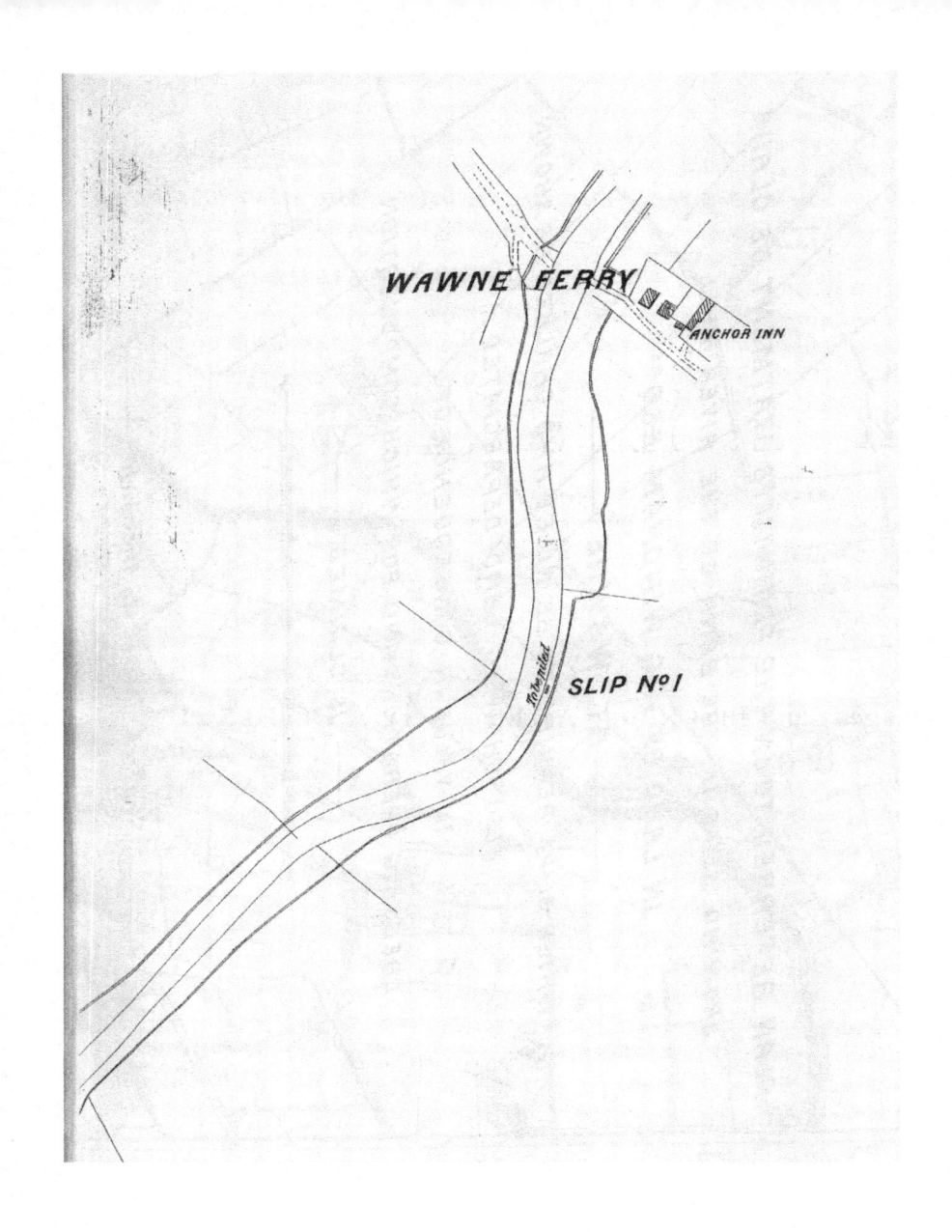

These complaints also involved the ferry. On the 15th October 1885 Windham's agent, Edward Knox wrote to the clerk of the Beverley and Barmston Drainage Commissioners (Henry Bainton) about the problems of the ferry. The letter bluntly requested that they do something about the landing stages at both sides of the ferry as "owing to your dredging operations you have made it impossible and at the same time very dangerous to work the ferry boat at low water." (72) Two days later Knox wrote again to say "I hope that you will see your way to doing something to the ferry landings as I am receiving constant complaints from people using it." (73) In April 1886 London solicitors acting for William George Windham alleged that the "dredging you have done in the River Hull has caused serious damage to the ferry and to the river banks among Mr Windham's lands." The Commissioners must have acknowledged some responsibility for on the 18th April 1886 Henry Bainton wrote to Edward Knox to say: "the commissioners deny that they have caused any damage to the ferry beyond what they have already paid compensation for." This legal wrangling dragged on until June 1888 but it seems likely that a new pontoon and chain ferry and new slipways at the Wawne and Thearne ferry crossings were purchased as a result of the compensation paid by the Beverley and Barmston Drainage Commissioners. It is unclear when the new chain ferry came into operation but it seems likely that it was built at a shipyard in Hull or Beverley. A drawing of Wawne Ferry by the artist Frederick Schultz Smith (that includes the new chain ferry) is dated 1896.

A similar "wagon ferry", chain operated, opened on the 23rd April 1884 upstream from Wawne at Grovehill, Beverley. It was built and operated by Thomas Harwood Harrison, the tenant of the Nag's Head Inn, which like the Anchor Inn / Windham Arms was situated on the river-bank. (74)

Image above: A drawing of Wawne Ferry by F S Smith (1896)

Standing in the Wawne punt either as a foot passenger or with a bicycle must have been a hazardous business (especially in windy conditions) since there were no guardrails. Travelling on the chain ferry could also be dangerous if the ferryman or his passengers did not take care. In 1899 local newspapers reported on a serious accident to a horse and trap en route from Beverley to Sutton on the evening of the 7th June. The four occupants of the trap included the driver, Mr H Webster, the landlord of the Duke of York Inn Sutton. (75) They had probably been to Beverley Races together and became involved in another "exciting experience" when they reached the Thearne side of the river. According to the Hull Daily Mail:

"The end of the boat was not quite parallel with the bank and the horse caught its foot between the two." (76)

The Beverley Guardian described what happened next: "It

appears that in descending the slope to the ferry the horse was unable to hold properly in check the conveyance with the result that it missed its footing on the boat, swerved and fell headlong into the river. The horse dragged after it the trap and two of its occupants who were immersed in the deep water but who luckily escaped without receiving any further harm. The horse however was drowned before it could be rescued." (77)

The Hull Daily Mail reported that "the trap is at present at the bottom of the river and will, it is feared, be an inconvenience to navigation." (78)

By 1895 John Wood worked at the ferry. In that year he showed great courage when he thwarted an attempted suicide there. On Sunday 26th May 1895 a middle aged woman called Emily Cousens from Hull tried to drown herself in the river. When she was chest high in the water, Wood went into the river to rescue her and then handed her over to the police. According to medical opinion of the time she was in "a low condition bodily and mentally" as the result of typhoid fever and "was not altogether accountable for her actions." (79) The unfortunate woman was committed, temporarily, to an asylum and on the 2nd June 1895 appeared before East Riding magistrates charged with attempting to commit suicide by walking into the River Hull near Wawne Ferry. The magistrates that day: Mr Hudson, Colonel Grimston, Alderman Burton and Mr Broadley Harrison, took an enlightened and sympathetic approach to the case. After hearing that Mrs Cousens was separated from her husband and was in a weak and dejected condition the magistrates handed her over the care of a niece who promised to look after her. (80)

The 1901 Census shows that John Wood was 47 years old and had four sons, aged thirteen, twelve, seven and three. (81) Also living at the Windham Arms at the time of the census were two servants, Frederick Wilkinson, a farm worker, aged seventeen (from Hessle) and Mary Thompson, a domestic servant, aged fourteen, from Cottingham.

From time immemorial the ferry had been worked using a small wooden boat or punt. By the 20th century this was described as being about 14ft long and 3ft wide and was operated by the ferryman using a stour about eight feet long. Standing at the rear of the boat he would use the stour to push the boat away from the landing and guide it across the river by pushing it against the river bed. Successive generations of skilled ferrymen learned how to judge the fickle tides and currents of the River Hull and use the stour so that the boat arrived at the opposite landing without mishap. The river could be fast flowing after periods of heavy rainfall upstream and great skill was needed when judging the current. As Jack Clarkson (1920-1996) who, from the age of fourteen, worked for Donald Brewer said "it was a work of art taking the ferry across the forty five feet of water which lay between one bank and the other." If the tide was flowing from Beverley to Hull, the ferryman would guide the boat away from the Wawne landing upstream and the tide would drift it back to the ferry landing on the west bank of the river. If the river was shallow enough the end of the stour could touch the river bed and be used to push the boat along. If, however, the river was in flood, "you had to give one almighty push and hope for the best since the stour would no nowhere near touch the bottom." (82) Using the stour to propel the ferryboat had been easier when the "ancient ford" was still in existence at the ferry crossing. However, following the dredging of the river in 1884, the operation of the punt was made more difficult at high tide.

The dangers of navigating the River Hull (for the inexperienced) are well illustrated by the story of twenty eight year old Frederick Robinson of Wilbert Lane, Beverley who drowned following a boating accident in April 1888. He had set out from Grovehill in a canoe on Saturday 14th April and made for Wawne Ferry. At the Windham Arms he had a bottle of porter while he waited for the tide to turn and then said goodnight "to Mr Brewer, the innkeeper, and the Wawne gamekeeper" before returning to his canoe. (83) However on the return trip he disappeared; his boat was found capsized near Weel the following day. (84) Despite some dragging of the river the body of Robinson was not found. Three men searching for him at Grovehill in the hope of a reward discovered the body of a sixty-year old woman called Waldron who had been missing for five months. (85) Despite the fact that the hands of the unfortunate woman were tied together the East Riding Coroner did not seem to regard the death as suspicious and recorded a verdict on her of "found drowned." (86)

    The introduction of the pontoon ferry must have increased the profits of Wawne Ferry since local farmers could now use it to move machinery, local traders to transport their goods by wagons and carts and the well-to-do of Wawne and perhaps Sutton to travel to Beverley by carriage / trap. However since Sutton-on-Hull had a regular train service to Hull from 1864, with connecting trains to Beverley, traffic across the river from this source must have been limited.

    The Wawne pontoon hauled manually across the River Hull by chains was typical of narrow waterways in the rural districts of England. In addition to Wawne and Grovehill there were numerous other examples of this type of ferry craft including those across the River Yare in Norfolk (the Loddon to Reedham Ferry) and over the Thames in Oxfordshire (the Bablockhythe Ferry). (87) The Wawne Pontoon Ferry was of a steel construction but with timber decking. Jack Clarkson, who worked the pontoon in the 1930s, recalls that there were two chains stretching from riverbank to riverbank through runners on the side of the pontoon. The chain used depended on the way the tide was flowing; if the tide was running from Beverley to Hull it was the right hand chain and if the tide was running from Hull to Beverley it was the left chain. The chain was pulled "hand over hand, sailor fashion" in order to draw the pontoon from the Wawne slipway to the Thearne side and occasionally it broke. (88) The Ferries Committee Report of 1948 was critical of this type of pontoon and chain ferry claiming "the use of chains stretching from bank to bank in busy waterways is open to objection because of the danger to navigation." (89) By the end of the nineteenth century the River Hull was extremely busy with keels, barges and other vessels travelling back and forth to Beverley and beyond as well as ships being built at the Beverley shipyards of Cook Gemmel and Welton and that of Joseph Scarr. Despite the dredging which had taken place at the ferry crossing in 1884 the operation of the pontoon could produce problems for other river users. When not in use the chain was supposed to lie slack on the riverbed so as not to obstruct navigation. However, at times this did not happen. Occasionally vessels using the river, like the barges employed by Hodgson's Tannery in Beverley, caught the chain and broke it forcing the ferryman to use the stour instead to propel the pontoon across the river. (90)

The attitude of the river authorities to such pontoon and chain ferries is illustrated by the attempts of a Mr G. Keeple and Mr E. Jellett get their permission for a new floating bridge about one mile south of Wawne Ferry (adjacent to Ings and Gibraltar Farms). The proposal was first made in 1911 (and again in 1913 and 1916) but had to be abandoned, partly because of the opposition of the Holderness Drainage Trustees and the Commission of Sewers. (91) However, there was nothing they could do in the case of Wawne Ferry since the ferry rights had been in existence and had been exercised for hundreds of years.

Image above: The punt in use to ferry cyclists in the 1890s

Image below: Police Constable Herbert Hobson in the punt around 1909

Despite the many changes of tenants, ownership of the ferry had remained in the hands of the Windham family since the beginning of the 18th century. Like many major landowners of the 1870's however the Windhams were affected by the depression in farming caused by growing foreign competition. An indenture of 6th May 1881 records that William George Windham mortgaged all his manors, farms tithes, etc and also "all that ferry over the River Hull." (92) He died on the 26th December 1887 at Bournemouth where he had been living for some years in failing health and only occasionally visiting his property in Yorkshire. Among those at the funeral was Edward Knox the agent for the Wawne Estate. (93) Since William George Windham died, childless, the estate passed to his brother Ashe Windham (1830-1909) and then to his nephew Ashe Windham Junior (1863-1937), a Captain in the East Yorkshire Regiment who had served with distinction in the Boer War. (94) The economic difficulties of the Windhams however continued to grow with the result that the entire Windham estate at Wawne was put up for sale on the 15th and 16th June 1911. (95) The effects on Wawne were profound: all the farmland (except Glebe Farm) together with blocks of cottages and shops were auctioned. (96)

Sales particulars from the auction of Friday 16th June 1911 show that Lot 42 was "the small and valuable property known as the Windham Arms comprising forty-three acres, inn and homestead (pasture and arable)." Included in lot 42 were the rights to and income from Wawne Ferry which at that time averaged about £52 per year from which there was an "annual payment of £7 13s 0d (less income tax) payable to the Lord of the Manor of the Beverley Water Towns." (97) A newspaper clipping from the time shows that the Windham Arms, its land and Wawne Ferry were sold that day for £2,100. (98) The purchaser was Donald Brewer who had been the tenant since 1907. By purchasing the ferry from the Windhams Donald Brewer now became solely responsible for the repair of the boats, the cleaning of the ferry-way in the river and the annual payment to the Lord of the Manor of the Beverley Water Towns for the use of the river bank on the Thearne side. One immediate effect of the change in ownership was soon apparent. Under the Windhams letters to Beverley were sent via the ferry at 4pm each day. (99) As *tenant* Donald Brewer was under agreement to the Windham family to ferry free of charge the postman and the Wawne school mistress but as *owner* he refused to ferry anyone for free. As a consequence the Post Office then arranged for all Wawne mail to be delivered from Sutton rather than from Beverley.(100) The 1911 Census shows that living with Donald Brewer at the Windham Arms were his wife Sarah (age 46), James Hardy (a 50 year old Farm labourer from Frodingham), Elsie Mariah Gibbins (a 14 year old domestic servant from Beverley) and John Henry Barrow (a 14 year old ferry and farm servant from Beverley).

Image above: Wawne Hall was created in the later 19th century for the Windham family out of a late 18th century farmhouse. Major Ashe Windham was the last of the family to live there in the 1920s. During the Second World War troops were billeted there and the house was demolished in the 1950s. (101)

Image above: Wawne's very muddy main street around 1900

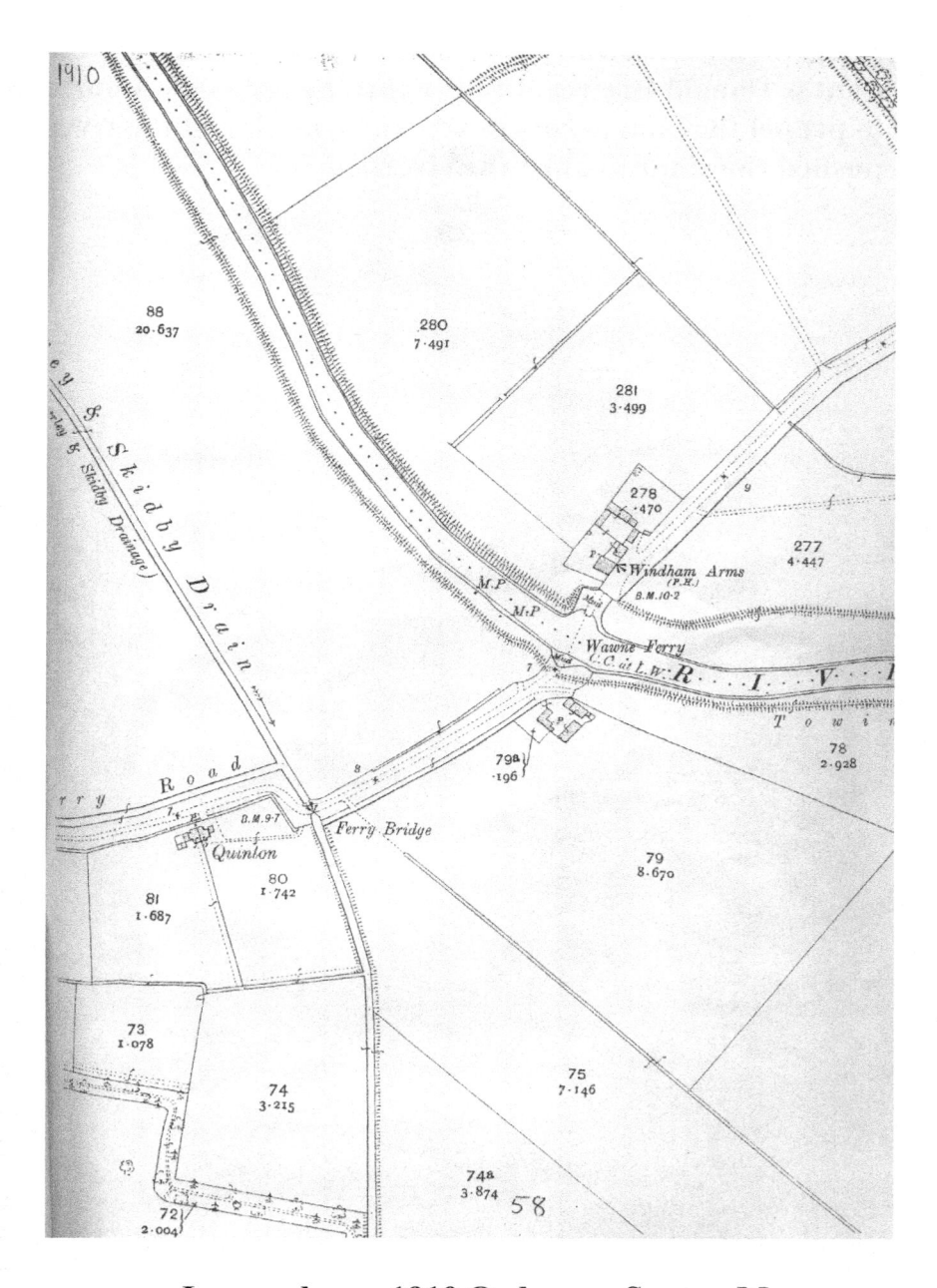

Image above: 1910 Ordnance Survey Map

Image below: Wawne Ferry around 1911. Standing in the punt is Donald Brewer. In his hands he holds the stour used to propel the boat across to the Thearne side of the river. He pushed the stour against the riverbed.

Image below: The pontoon ferry at Wawne. The ferryman pulled on a chain to move the pontoon across the river to the Thearne side.

Chapter Three: Within Living Memory

Although no figures survive on the use of Wawne Ferry by the public newspaper accounts provide us with some clues, A 'Holderness Letter' article by "Paul Pry" in a September 1914 issue of the Hull Daily Mail claimed that a bridge at Wawne Ferry was still possible and that "there are some individuals and some official bodies who are very strong on the scheme and who believe that such a project would be not only feasible, but financially a good investment." He went on to say that "at the present time there is not such a very large volume of traffic across the ferry" but that this could change "if a bridge were provided instead of the present cumbrous system of crossing the river."

Ferries in England and Wales: RAC Guide and Handbook 1927-1928 (p.342)

Beverley-Sutton (Yorks)- Wawne Ferry

At all states of the tide (except very low tide, when short delay occurs), from 6am to 10pm; weekday and Sunday service. Cars (small), 6d; motor cycles 4d; passengers 1d. Advisable to give notice beforehand if several cars are crossing.

The rise of the motor vehicle at first provided increased opportunities for the ferry but in the long term was to prove its undoing. In the days of horse drawn transport when time mattered less the ferry provided a valuable link between Beverley and the villages east of the River Hull, particularly Sutton-on-Hull. However as motor transport became predominant Wawne Ferry became irrelevant. The main centres of population were Hull and Beverley and neither of them needed the ferry.

In the context of the national decline of river ferries, the Ferries Committee report of 1948 produced statistics on the use of mechanically propelled vehicles. During the period 1922-1939 they increased nationally by 231%. Of this increase the most significant was that of private motorcars which increased by 546% and goods vehicles by 223%. (1) Locally the Hull to Beverley Road (the A1079) was the busiest of the six Class A roads leaving Hull averaging "5,364 vehicles of all classes per day during the census of 1935." (2) The greatest concentration of traffic occurred on Sundays during the holiday months "when over 9,200 vehicles have been counted at Plaxton Bridge between 6am and 10pm." The 1920s and 1930s were also an age of cycling and this same 1935 census records that there were 2000 cyclists using the A1079 per day. The Wawne Ferry punt carried numerous cyclists back and forth over the river at 2d per time. (3) However, the inconvenience of the pontoon, especially the delays experienced at the Thearne side when waiting for the ferryman meant that it was little used by cars. The cobbled landing ramp at the Thearne side of the river when muddy could cause problems for cars using it. If their tyres were wet "with a little bit of mud on them, they would get nearly to the top and then slide back to the bottom again" (4)

Rupert Alec Smith spent his early years at Wawne Lodge and travelled in the large family motorcar on trips over Wawne Ferry for which the ferryman was paid 1 shilling. He said "it was our usual custom to take the car over the ferry for our journeys to Beverley, but later we learned that it was really quicker to go by the very twisting Meaux Lane from Wawne to Routh and from there to Beverley." (5)

Despite its limited use by motor vehicles there were some accidents at or near Wawne Ferry. In January 1922 the Yorkshire Evening Post reported that:

"A motorist was apparently a stranger to the district when

passing through the village of Wawne. Unaware of the river and ferry he failed to slacken his speed and the car plunged into the river and sank in mid-stream. The driver whose identity is not disclosed, saved himself by jumping out and swimming to the landing stage. A horse was used to salvage the car at low tide." (6)

In 1936, west of Wawne Ferry, a car being driven by a Mrs Simpson of Hull was "proceeding from Wawne Ferry Lane" on to the main road when she collided with a motorcyclist at the Woodmansey crossroads. The motorcyclist was then knocked into a lorry with "machine and rider becoming wedged underneath." The rider Henry Holdroyd (aged 17) was taken to the Hull Royal Infirmary with foot injuries. (7)

In September 1938, a Hull man (Ralph Hamilton Hangar) was convicted of "driving under the influence of drink" at a court in Beverley and fined £15 including costs. He had been driving from Wawne Ferry towards Wawne village when he collided with a woman cyclist and then with a bridge. (8)

Other more tragic events took place at Wawne Ferry with deaths from accidents. In 1907 Donald Brewer was called to give evidence at a coroners inquest into the death of Fred Fishers, age 20, the son of a coachman of Woodmansey. Brewer had found Fisher's body in the river near Wawne Ferry. The jury returned an open verdict of "found drowned." (9) Five years later Donald Brewer was called to give evidence again at an inquest. This time it was into the death of Charles Henry Fox, a sixty-one year old engine driver from Hull whose body was recovered from the river after he had been missing for two weeks. Brewer had seen the victim (a keen walker) pass the Windham Arms on the evening of Sunday 14th April. Fox was walking along the river with his dogs in the direction of Stoneferry and Brewer suggested that that bank here was so steep that "if anyone got into the water it would not be easy to get out again."

Other bodies were found in the river at Wawne Ferry in August 1935 and January 1938. In the latter case Donald Brewer found the body of Harry Philip Oakes, a thirty-one year old Driffield grocer, floating in the river on January 20th 1938. At the inquest, held before the Holderness Coroner in the Windham Arms, a verdict of "found drowned" was returned. (10)

An article in the Hull Daily Mail on the 1st June 1922, if unrepresentative of the annual use of Wawne Ferry, shows how popular it could be in the summer months of the inter-war years. The reporter wrote:

"Smoking a contemplative evening pipe whilst sitting on the wall at Wawne Ferry, I was interested in the amount of traffic which finds its way across this ferry. The other evening, inside an hour, the traffic taken across included a large 4-seater car, a motorcycle and sidecar, a racehorse, a pony and trap and any number of cyclists. Some people might not take a motor vehicle over the river to get to Beverley, but the saving of even a few miles and time is valuable at times. The Kingston Rowing Club members on the river, the boy scouts in camp using the round huts formerly occupied by the military and the panoramic view of the countryside: all add to the interest of this sylvan river spot. A refresher at the old Windham Arms may also appeal to some."

In addition to the long-term threat to Wawne Ferry posed by the motorcar there were other dangers. Communication between Wawne, Sutton and Hull became easier with the introduction of bus services in the 1920's. Neil Thompson of Sutton, a bus operator. was asked by residents of Wawne in 1923 to start a service to Hull via Sutton. This operated three days a week and was taken over by East Yorkshire Motor Services when they bought his business in October 1926. (11) By the late 1930's Hull Corporation buses were operating to and from Wawne on

Tuesdays and Saturdays. (12) At a time when few people owned a car bus services made Hull a more popular destination than Beverley. To get to Beverley via the A1079 required a ferry trip and a walk of about one and a half miles.

As we have seen there was a growing use of Wawne Ferry and its peaceful River Hull location for leisure by boy scouts and others. At a general meeting of the 'Hull Scouts' in April 1920 it was said:

"The site acquired at Wawne Ferry would be difficult to improve upon. Within a reasonable distance to the city, the ferry is easily accessible to Troops of all divisions. Moreover, the position is healthy commanding an excellent view of the Wolds, Beverley Minster and surrounding country."

Walking was a popular pastime during the inter-war years and an issue of the Hull Daily Mail (July 23rd 1932) recommended a route that included Wawne Ferry. Called "weekend hikes from Hull" the article said: "after a series of stiles the next place is Wawne Ferry connecting the Sutton side with the Beverley side. Motor boats, house boats and an occasional keel under sail add interest to the river."

The popularity of the River Hull is demonstrated by the increasing number of houseboats moored at or near Wawne Ferry and the use of a field adjacent to the Windham Arms for tents /caravans / holiday homes in the 1920s and 1930s. Mrs Joan Tasker of Hessle recalls that as a child her family took her to a "round corrugated iron hut at Wawne Ferry" for weekends. Not having a car they took the bus up Beverley Road to Thearne Lane and then walked along it to the ferry. She also recalls being taken on an outing and picnic to Wawne Ferry while a pupil at Newland High School, Hull. Alf Mann of Skipsea recalls that his father Tommy Mann had a houseboat moored on the riverbank close to the Windham Arms in the mid 1930s. An advertisement in the Hull Daily for May 9th 1921 told readers:

" For Sale, excellent House Boat 33ft by 9ft, with two cabins, accommodation for 6; fitted ready for cruising – Apply Brewer, Wawne Ferry."

Boating however was not without its dangers. Local newspapers reported on an incident in January 1935 involving Charles Walgate a Hull man. He was seriously injured in a shooting accident on a houseboat, The Hull Daily Mail said: "Walgate was one of a party of four on a houseboat moored at Wawne Ferry when another member of the party picked up a gun with the intention of shooting a bird. The gun went off accidentally and the shot entered Walgate's thigh." He later died at Hull Royal Infirmary.

Image below: A deserted Wawne Ferry showing the punt and the pontoon. The photograph is probably from the 1920s

Image above: Wawne Ferry became a popular place for leisure in the 1920s and 1930s. Boys (possibly scouts) can be seen using the pontoon for swimming.

Wawne Ferry and the Windham Arms were popular places for weekend visitors. Jack Clarkson recalls that on one Bank Holiday Monday in June he took eighteen shillings from foot passengers and cyclists in ferry tolls. These visitors also improved the income of the Windham Arms where "we used to make nearly as much of what we call back door trade, crisps, chocolate, cigarettes and lemonade, as we could in the pub at the weekend." The Windham Arms was open each day from 11am to 2pm and from 7pm to 10pm; the ferry acted as a kind of shuttle service for customers on the west bank of the river. (13) In order to compete with rival public houses (like the Coach and Horses and the Ship in Dunswell or the Dixons Arms in Woodmansey) customers travelling to and from the Windham Arms were ferried free of charge. (14) Donald Brewer was well aware of his competitive disadvantage compared to the public houses in Dunswell and Woodmansey. These were open on Sundays for the sale of alcohol 'on the premises', whereas he was only allowed to make 'off sales'. Therefore Donald Brewer applied for a new licence for 'Sunday on-sales' in March 1922. This new licence was approved by the 'Licensing Sessions of the North Hunsley Division.' (15) The Windham Arms consisted of one large room with bare wooden tables lit by paraffin lamps. The John Smith's beers for sale were dispensed from wooden barrels laid on their side. (16)

The Brewers had no children and with a farm, a public house and a ferry to run they employed others to help them. In the 1920s one of these was Robert Cherry of Bewholme Grove, Hull.(17) In May 1922 Sarah Brewer advertised for a "Country Girl (14-15) for general work." (18) Mrs B Cawood of Flamborough (but formerly of Wawne) remembers doing this work, as a girl of fourteen, when she cycled to the Windham Arms each day for an 8am start. Her duties, between 1929 and 1932, included general housework, serving customers and churning cream into butter. She said: "Friday was butter making day and I had to carry buckets of cream to the dairy and tip them into the churn. After the churning was complete, Mrs Brewer came and made the butter into pounds and half pounds."

Even in the 1920s farming was labour intensive with harvest time particularly busy. An item in the Hull Daily Mail (September 17th 1920) reported "Mr Donald Brewer of Wawne Ferry and Mr Robert Swift of Wawne Common have got all their corn safely gathered in and stacked." Ferry Farm was a mix of arable and pasture with Donald Brewer keeping cows, pigs and poultry. In 1934 he was advertising "Turkey eggs for sale at one shilling each." (19) As a young man Arthur Swift of Wawne Common Farm kept a diary and in 1922 wrote: "Went to wash sheep at the ferry. Put fence across the ferryboat. Mr Brewer pulled them out with a boat hook." (20)

The regular customers of the ferry were those trades people and professionals who lived at one side of the River Hull and worked at the other side. Jack Clarkson recalled that the ferry operated from about 6 am although the first passengers were usually farm workers employed at Kenley Farm who arrived at the Thearne side at about 6.30am.

Mrs Jean Davies of Willerby records that in 1932, at the age of 10, she moved from Beverley to Wawne when her mother was appointed headteacher of Wawne School. For several months she continued her education in Beverley and was ferried across the river each day by Donald Brewer.

" I left home in Wawne at 8am and cycled one mile to Wawne Ferry. At low tide he took me and my cycle across the river in the punt but at high tide he often used the raft and pulled the chains." (21)

Alf Mann, born 1930, remembers attending Wawne Village School for two years when his family: "were bombed out of Hull". He recalls that they had an elderly teacher called Miss

Moses who lived in Thearne and cycled to school each day crossing over the river on the ferry "in all weathers without mishap and was never late."

Molly Moore and her twin sister Nancy (born 1920) lived at Sicey Cottage in Woodmansey and used the ferry to visit an aunt who lived in Wawne. They used their bikes to cycle down Thearne Lane to the ferry before shouting "boat" to attract the ferryman's attention. Nancy Moore recalled that a farmer at Thearne used the ferry regularly to "go across for his pint at the Windham Arms until he fell for the barmaid causing his marriage to break up and a real scandal."

Traders used the ferry too. In the late 19th century there was 'Tin Hat Man' who lived on a houseboat on the Thearne side of the river. He used the ferry to supply Wawne with items like lace, handkerchiefs, bootlaces and buttons. (22) In the twentieth century the pontoon was in use to carry the horse and cart of Mr Snow who on Mondays delivered butter, eggs and curd to homes on the Wawne side of the river. (23) Other regular customers of the ferry were two butchers: Tommy Watson and Neville Hardy. Neville Hardy lived in Beverley and used the ferry on Tuesdays and Fridays to transport his horse and cart to the Wawne side. (24)

Image above: Cyclists crossing the river in the 1920s or 1930s

Image above: The same cyclists arriving at the Wawne side. On a good day the crossing of this narrow river could be done in minutes.

Local farmers sometimes used the pontoon for transporting animals. Jack Clarkson recalls that the owners of Ings Farm at Wawne travelled around local markets on a Saturday buying cattle and transported these by lorry to the Thearne side of the river. From here the pontoon took them to the Wawne side at five shillings a load. Ings Farm lay close to the river bank and so it was convenient to move animals in this way. However, with the increased use of lorries for moving cattle it is obvious that the use of the pontoon would have declined in the long term. The days when cattle and sheep were transported over the ferry to the west bank and driven along the drovers road (German Nook Lane) to Figham Pastures (Beverley) were long gone. (25) However, there was still some use of the pontoon in the 1920s and 1930s for moving the occasional pony and trap at 6d a time, for moving farm machinery and to transport the Holderness

Hunt. (26)

There were meetings of the Holderness Hunt at Wawne Ferry in both the nineteenth and twentieth centuries. Even before the introduction of the pontoon ferry c. 1890 a boat was used to transport hunt members and the foxhounds across the river. The Hull Packet of 22nd February 1867 described "another great run with the Holderness foxhounds" and said:

" On Monday 11th February, the meet was at the village of Wawne. The morning was bright and fine with a stiffish westerly breeze. The hounds were late in coming, as the ferryboat at Wawne had been swamped in the night and was lying at the bottom of the river, so they had to go round (5 or 6 miles) by Hull Bridge. Several sportsmen who did not know of the accident to the boat until they reached the river's brink, were left behind altogether."

There were further weather problems in 1895 when it was reported that that meet of the Holderness Hounds was "very much interfered with by the storm". When the pack arrived at the Thearne side the river was like a sea with "the waves running very high. To get across was a work of great difficulty. Ash managed to get the hounds over with a good deal of trouble and some of the horsemen followed. The others returned home." (27)
The result was that the meeting had to be abandoned. (28)

Images: Transporting the Holderness Hunt from the Thearne side of the river. Photographs probably from the 1920s

By the turn of the twentieth century Wawne Lodge (built around 1890) had become one of the principal meets of the Holderness Hunt.[29] In its early years the Lodge was occupied by Ashe Windham Junior, Captain of the 3rd Battalion of the East Yorkshire Regiment (30) and son of Ashe Windham Senior who lived at Wawne Hall. Members of the Holderness
Hunt were divided geographically by the River Hull into Wolds members on the west and Holderness members on the east. Between 1878 and 1914 all the Masters of the Holderness Hunt lived to the west of the River Hull. Arthur Wilson of Tranby Croft was Master between 1878 and 1905, followed by Charles Brook of the Hall, Cherry Burton (1905-1908) and finally Mr H. Whitworth of Scorboro (1909-1914).(31) As a huntsman himself Captain Windham made the Wawne Ferry pontoon available to the Wolds members of the Hunt to cross the river with their horses and foxhounds. Jack Clarkson recalled that in the 1930s he brought across "four or five fellows on horses in white breaches and red jackets" but that one of the horses shied and sent its rider into the river mud. (32)

Image above: a meeting of the Holderness Hunt in the early 20th century

In the late 1930s two school teachers called Miss Johnson and Miss Skaife who lived at Beverley cycled to the Thearne side of the ferry each day. Leaving their cycles at Prospect Farm they would then be ferried across the river for work at Wawne School and in the evening would be ferried back again for their return trip to Beverley. (33)

      The punt remained the mainstay of the ferry service in the 1930s and during the years of the Second World War. Passengers arriving at the Thearne side of the river had to ring a bell to attract the attention of Donald Brewer or one of his assistants. (34) When the bell was later stolen would-be passengers had to shout the word "boat" to attract the attention of the ferryman at the Windham Arms. In fact, the boat could sometimes be slow in coming either because Donald Brewer was busy elsewhere on the farm or in the Windham Arms or because he preferred to wait until there was more than one passenger to ferry. (35) The punt could hold four or five people or two persons with cycles and all passengers had to stand since there were no seats. (36) With the absence of any protective side rails the ferry could provide a terrifying experience for passengers especially on a stormy winter's night when the crossing was done in total darkness. As Jack Clarkson commented "if the wind and tide were both going the same way…it were a rum job to get across." Once, in the teeth of a gale, he had to ferry the parson across the river from the Thearne side. "The parson had to hold his hat on because it was blowing so hard" and the wind drove the punt to Wawne Landing downstream from the ferry dock.

Image above: Wawne Ferry at low tide

Image above: The pontoon ferry with the Windham Arms and its farm buildings in the background

Chapter Four: Demise

Sarah Brewer suffered from diabetes and died on the 3rd May 1939 (37) leaving Donald Brewer alone to run the ferry, farm and public house with whatever help he could find. One of those who worked for him during the war years was Annie Hinch. With the coming of the Second World War in September 1939 the punt ferry continued in use and gained new passengers when Wawne Hall was requisitioned for use by the military. Annie Hinch recalled that soldiers and ATS girls from Wawne Hall used the Windham Arms, the only public house in Wawne, for drinking and social gatherings "especially on Thursday when they got paid." The Hall and other buildings in the grounds became the headquarters of the anti-aircraft batteries along the north bank of the Humber. (38) These same service personnel enjoyed trips to Beverley at weekends. They faced a long walk from the village to the ferry in order to cross the river and then another walk of about a mile along Ferry Lane and Thearne Lane to the nearest bus stop on the Hull to Beverley Road. (39) Sometimes, to the annoyance of Donald Brewer, these soldiers decided to create mischief by untying the ferryboat and letting it float downstream. (40) The ferry was also used by Land Girls travelling to farms on both sides of the river. However the authorities ordered the houseboats and other craft moored near Wawne Ferry to be moved thereby removing a source of revenue from the Windham Arms and the ferry. (41) It may be an indication of the effect the war had curtailing the leisure business at the ferry in that that the following advertisement appeared in the Hull Daily Mail on the 3st May 1940: "For Sale, Bungalow; Wawne Ferry- Apply Wyndham Arms, Wawne Ferry."

The area around Wawne had long been a favourite place of the military for training or war games. The Beverley Guardian of August 25th 1888 reported on a "volunteer sham fight at Wawne" and said "the success of the recent route march and sham fight at Wawne between the A and B companies of the Hull Rifle Corps led to a second experiment in this direction." This took place on Saturday 18th August 1888 and began with a parade at Londesborough Barracks in Hull where blank ammunition was distributed. The exercise was a fight between the rearguard of an enemy that was supposed to be retreating by way of Wawne Ferry and the advancing guards of the attacking force approaching from Sutton-on-Hull. At the end of the exercise the volunteers crossed over the river on the ferry and marched back to Hull by way of Beverley Road. Another of these war games took place at Wawne Ferry in 1898 in which we are told "the operations were seriously impeded by the large numbers of the public who were there." (42) Since this had long been an important crossing place on the river it was perhaps for strategic reasons that a military camp was established near Wawne Ferry during the First World War. To allow for troop movements over the river a military bridge was constructed a little downstream of the ferry crossing. In 1919 the Highways and Bridges Committee of East Yorkshire Council considered a letter from the Lord Lieutenant of the East Riding asking them if the County Council wished to take over the "emergency" bridge for civilian use. The Council declined the offer. (43)

Image above: The military bridge of World War One with the pontoon ferry in the foreground.

In March 1921 a contributor to the Hull Daily Mail questioned why this military bridge had not been retained. He wrote:

"The other day I had occasion to cross the river Hull at Wawne and, as it happened, I had not been over there since the days of the war. Now it is giving no secrets away now, to ask why on earth that wooden bridge that spanned the river at Wawne Ferry during the war should not have been allowed to remain for peacetime purposes? It was a strong serviceable structure apparently, although I never saw it used, so why could not this eminently desirable and much needed improvement have been allowed to remain. The crossing of the ferry is not without its danger, although every precaution is taken, but there are people who would rather go round by Hull or Routh to get to Beverley from Wawne. (44)

Image above: Military bridge of World War Two

Another "military bridge" was constructed at the same place during World War Two. Brian Newlove of Hall Farm Thearne remembers as a boy watching contractors driving piles into the riverbank to support the span. This timber bridge was a low structure with the centre section removable to allow for the movement of ships to and from Beverley. Molly Moore married Tom Rodmell of Sicey Farm Woodmansey in 1940 and remembers watching the bridge being built. She said: "when they finished it they drove a couple of lorries over it to test it." On the 1st October 1945 the Highways and Bridges Committee of East Yorkshire Council considered a similar letter to that of 1919. This time the enquiry was from Councillor H. Mackrill who wished to know, at the request of the parishioners of Wawne, if the Council would consider buying "the timber trestle structure erected by the military authorities".(45) The offer was once more declined and so the bridge was dismantled.

Despite the wartime use of the punt for ferrying foot passengers and cyclists it seems the pontoon was by now used rarely. Explanations have been put forward for this. It has been claimed that the pontoon sank, the victim of a German bomb (46). ARP records show that there was bombing in the vicinity of Wawne Ferry in both March and July 1941. On the 18th, 19th and 24th March 1941 a number of bombs fell in the Wawne and Thearne areas including Glebe Farm on the Wawne side and Sicey Farm on the Thearne side. A message to the Air Raid Control Centre in Beverley also reported a loud explosion 300 yards north of Wawne Ferry caused by a parachute mine. This damaged the riverbanks on both sides of the River Hull but according to the police there was no other damage or casualties. (47) Six high explosive bombs were also dropped in the vicinity of Wawne Ferry early in the morning of July 17th 1941. However, they were dropped on the Thearne side and according to official records caused no casualties and did no damage. (48)

A more likely explanation for the increasing redundancy of the pontoon ferry was a limited demand for the service it provided after 1937 combined with petrol rationing during the Second World War. Petrol rationing was first introduced on the 23rd September 1939, within three weeks of the outbreak of the war, to ensure that the military and other essential services given the first priority in allocating scarce fuel supplies. On the 1st July 1942 the basic civilian petrol ration was abolished altogether making fuel unobtainable for the private car. Many car owners mothballed their vehicles for the duration of the war.

However the decline of the chain ferry service had already started during 1937, two years before the outbreak of war. As more bridges were built downstream of Wawne and motor transport decreased travel times between Beverley and Hull so the viability of the ferry was increasingly under threat. The building of new bridges on the lower reaches of the River Hull had already served to make other ferries redundant (like that at

Stoneferry). A new bridge at Drypool south of North Bridge had been sanctioned by Parliament in 1886. Built at a cost of £24,800 it was opened in 1889. (49) Upstream from North Bridge lay Sculcoates Bridge (1875), Scott Street Bridge (1902) and Stoneferry Bridge (1905).

Most serious for the future of Wawne Ferry, however, was Sutton Road Bridge. The parish of Sutton was affected by the suburban growth of Hull from the turn of the twentieth century. From the 1920's new housing estates had appeared in the south of the parish along the newly built Gillshill Road, James Reckitt Avenue and Sutton Road. (50) Authorised by an act of Parliament in 1934 the contract for the new Sutton Bridge was awarded to the Cleveland Bridge Company (part of the steel and engineering group Dorman Long of Middlesbrough). The bridge, costing £51,000, was the final link in Hull's new ring-road stretching from the north of the city to the docks in the east and was formally opened by Captain Austin Hudson MP, Parliamentary Secretary to the Minister of Transport on July 8th 1937. (51) As he unlocked the gates of the new bridge surrounded by Hull's proud civic elite Hudson announced: "I declare this bridge and road open for the free use of the King's subjects for ever." With the opening of Sutton Road and Sutton Road Bridge travel between Beverley, Woodmansey, Dunswell and places on the eastern side of the River Hull (including Sutton and Wawne) became a great deal easier. The new Sutton Road Bridge was only three miles downstream from Wawne Ferry. In effect, the pontoon and chain ferry at Wawne was by-passed by the use of the motor vehicle and the bridge. The drivers of cars, vans and lorries could use the new bridge for nothing but to use the Wawne pontoon ferry would, as well as delays, cost them between sixpence and a shilling depending on the size of the vehicle.

Lionel Heathcote who spent much time at the Windham Arms during 1938-1939 says "I never saw it in use". Alf Mann who as a schoolboy used the punt (1941) to cross to his family home in Wawne says that the pontoon was laid up at the river bank and semi-covered in river silt. This is confirmed by John Beaulah of Wawne who used the punt for trips to Thearne and Beverley early in the war and says that the pontoon had become merely a kind of "stepping stone" to get into the punt .

   With the opening of Hull's new bridge the use of the Wawne Pontoon Ferry became increasingly rare. Its use seems to have become restricted to those farmers and agricultural contractors living close to the river and who wished to move farm machinery. One example was Mark Jackson who lived in a cottage at Thearne and was an agricultural contractor. He owned a Fordson tractor that was in demand for work on farms in the Wawne / Sutton area (for example, Frog Hall Farm). During the war years he continued to use the pontoon to move his tractor back and forth across the river. (52) Another example was Geoffrey Newlove of Hall Farm Thearne. He also had the tenancy of Grange Croft Farm on the Wawne side of the River Hull and used the pontoon ferry to transport farm machinery. Hall Farm Thearne was less than half a mile from the ferry but it is significant that when his cattle had to be transported from Thearne to Wawne Geoffrey Newlove used a lorry and went by Sutton Road Bridge rather than the ferry. (53) Like other pontoon ferries elsewhere in England, the death of the Wawne Pontoon Ferry was a lingering one rather than a deliberate act of closure.

Image above: Sutton Road Bridge opened to traffic in July 1937. It was only three miles downstream from Wawne Ferry.

Image above: Thearne Hall was the home of Ronald Dixon who fought to have Wawne Ferry reinstated after it closed in August 1946.

The redundancy of the Wawne pontoon ferry was not unique in this respect: the Ferries Committee of the Ministry of Transport (1948) reported on thirteen pontoon and chain ferries (manually operated) of the type used at Wawne. Of these thirteen vehicle ferries, eight were no longer in operation by 1947. (54) The problems of the Surlingham-Postwick pontoon ferry in Norfolk (which closed in February 1946) were typical of the time. The landlord of the Ferry House Inn at Surlingham who operated it said that the weekly income of the ferry was under two pounds which was "insufficient to pay even one man's wages" and that the pontoon was rotten and unsafe to use.(55) The Ferries Committee heard evidence from its owners: the brewery company of Youngs, Crawshay and Youngs that the pontoon had been leaking "and needed constant pumping to keep it in a river-worthy condition." They pointed out that the ferry was little used and it would take an estimated £500 to restore it. (56)

The mid to late 1940s were a time of crisis for Britain's

smaller river ferries with their use declining and wage costs rising. In a similar situation to the Wawne pontoon, though still operating regularly, was the Southrey Ferry which crossed the River Witham and linked unclassified roads in Kesteven and Lindsey (Lincolnshire). The ferry was owned by the brewers Inde Coope and let to the tenant of the White Horse Inn. In 1947 it was estimated that only three vehicles per week used it. (57) The only regular passengers seemed to be early morning workmen, eight schoolchildren paid for by Kesteven Council and people using Southrey railway station.

The Wawne punt was used more often than the pontoon in the war years. Brian Newlove remembers, as a boy, making the short trip from the Thearne side so that he could get to Grange Croft Farm to check on his father's cattle for a condition called 'summer mastitis'. He said: "I went over there at weekends with a friend called Harry Lloyd to check the cows and sometimes called in at the Windham Arms for a shandy on the way back. I also saw Wawne schoolchildren using the ferry. They were scholarship pupils at Beverley Grammar School and Beverley High School and used the ferry to get to the Thearne side with their bikes. They would then cycle up Thearne Lane and leave their bikes in a shed at the top of the lane before catching the bus into Beverley. Some people living in Thearne, like Jim Rispin and Joan Blyth, used the ferry to go for a drink in the Windham Arms." (58)

By 1941 Donald Brewer was employing a wartime evacuee from Hull to help him run the ferry and the farm. To escape the German bombing the Hanwell family had moved to a large caravan on the riverbank close to the Windham Arms. One of their young sons, Billy Hanwell, became a ferryman and "was expert with the stour." (59)

Image above: Bob Wray of Prospect Farm Thearne crossing the river with farm machinery in the late 1930s or early 1940s

Donald Brewer was, by 1941, seventy years old and with no children to help him he relied on paid employees, a limited resource in the war years, to assist in running the ferry, the farm and the Windham Arms. An advertisement in the Hull Daily Mail from October 4th 1943 might indicate the problems he faced. This said: "Wawne Ferry, Tuesday evening next at quarter to six pm at the Ferry Farm Wawne. Tom Jackson will sell by auction one and a half acres of growing crop mangolds at the Field Gate, the property of Mr D Brewer." Perhaps under pressure from the authorities to keep the ferry in operation for the movement of military personnel based in Wawne Donald Brewer called on his family for help. Harold Walker was the son of his sister, Mary Ellen Brewer (born in Arnold in 1864) and her husband Guy Walker. Harold Walker had been born in Arnold in 1899 but after 1911 was living in Bromley, Kent with his parents. In a conveyance dated 1st May 1944 Brewer transferred the ownership of the Windham Arms and the ferry to his nephew. (60) Although the forty-five year old Walker enjoyed working the farm and the Windham Arms he found the ferry duties "irksome and onerous" and grumbled to people about it. (61) The annoyance caused by shouts of "boat" at all hours of the day and evening, especially when he was engaged in milking or serving in the Windham Arms, can only be imagined. However it is possible that he was given some help by his uncle since the 1946 electoral register shows that Donald Brewer, now aged 76, was still living at the Windham Arms at that time.

Harold Walker's ownership of the Windham Arms and Wawne Ferry was not to last long. After only two years he sold both to Moors' and Robson's Ltd, a brewery company based in Hull, for £3000. The purchase, agreed on the 5th July 1946, included the ferry rights, forty-four and a half acres of land and growing crops which the "in-going tenant had agreed to purchase" (62). The sale was completed in a conveyance dated 19th August 1946. One of Harold Walker's final acts at the Windham Arms was to auction off all the livestock, machinery and equipment of Ferry Farm on Saturday 10th August 1946. The auction, carried out by F. Farnaby and Son of Wawne, included two horses, three heifers, two calves, three pigs, one hundred head fowls, fourteen ducks and seventy chicks. Also in the sale were a "strong cart, a new turnip cutter, an end-over-end churn, various huts and hen houses and surplus furniture including a piano." (63)

Wawne Ferry had, by 1946, existed for over 800 years. It was the departure of Harold Walker and Donald Brewer that marked the end of an era. One of the very last people to operate the punt was probably Tom Botham (1923-1994), a farm labourer in the Wawne area who worked for Harold Walker as a ferryman. Moors' and Robson's Brewery offered the tenancy of the Windham Arms to Tom Botham but he turned it down because the deal did not include Donald Brewer's caravan and camping field that had been so popular in the 1930s. However, as a final favour he ferried a hen party across the river in the summer of 1946 and awaited their return from Beverley. (64) This was probably the last time the ferryboat was used although the place name "Wawne Ferry" continued to be quoted in advertisements for some years after.

In the event the tenant chosen by Moors' and Robson's was Walter Twidale who moved into the Windham Arms with his wife Florence. (65) Walter Twidale had been born in Sutton in 1908 and was a relative of Donald Brewer. His father, Joseph Luke Twidale, a farmer, had married Donald Brewer's sister (Rebecca Kate Brewer, born 1872). (66) In 1946 Walter Twidale was 38 years old. In 1943 he had married Florence Lamming (born 1911) and they went on to have three children together: Maureen (born 1944), Nancy (born 1946) and Gwendoline (born 1948). (67)

It seems to have been the sale of the Windham Arms to Moors' and Robson's Brewery and the arrival of Walter Twidale (in late August 1946) which marked the final demise of Wawne Ferry. Many sources claim that the ferry closed in 1947 and at least one says that it was in the 1950s. (68) However, protests about the closure of the ferry had already begun by the end of 1946. Prominent among the protestors was Ronald Dixon (1873-1960) tenant of Thearne Hall and chairman of Woodmansey Parish Council.

Ronald Audley Martineau Dixon had been born in Hull and was the son of James Dixon, a Unitarian minister. At the time of the 1881 Census he was living with his parents, a brother and three sisters at 8 Dover Street, Sculcoates, Hull. Ten years later his father had died and his mother, Nanciebella, was described as "living on her own means as a widow". Living with her were Ronald and his younger brother Arnold who were both working as manufacturing clerks. Ronald Dixon was clearly a man of talent and intellect for by 1922 he was a Fellow of the Geological Society, a Fellow of the Royal Geographical Society and a Fellow of the Society of Antiquaries of London. This was a rare honour indicating that he "excelled in the knowledge of antiquities and history." By this time Dixon was a man of independent means too for the 1922 telephone directory shows that he was living at Wolfreton Hall, Kirkella. (69)

By 1927 he was the tenant of Thearne Hall and his interest in Wawne Ferry was shown when he wrote an article for the Hull Daily Mail on the subject of Sir John Hotham and his attempted escape via the "Thearne-Wawne ford or ferry." (70) As a historian Ronald Dixon was well aware that the closure of Wawne Ferry in late August 1946 was a significant historical event for this "passage over the River Hull" had been in existence for over eight hundred years, He therefore became a champion of the ferry and fought a long, but ultimately, losing battle to have it reinstated. We also have Dixon to thank for providing the information about the closure of the ferry through his entries in the Woodmansey Parish Council Minutes when local newspapers largely ignored the event.

A vigorous and committed campaigner, Dixon contacted the Yorkshire Parish Councils Association, Wawne Parish Council and Moor's and Robsons' Brewery. In reply to his letter, Moors' and Robson's claimed that the reason why the ferry had closed was that their tenant considered that the ferryboat was not safe to use and that the cost of repairing or replacing it was too excessive in view of the revenue it would generate. (71) In fact the high cost of repairing ferryboats compared with the amount of traffic using them was often given as the reason for abandoning river ferries at this time. (72) Given the experience of similar river ferries elsewhere in the country it is therefore likely that the weekly income of the ferry at the time of its closure was minimal. It seems that the only regular income of the ferry was the transport of those Wawne schoolchildren, each morning and afternoon, attending Beverley schools. During the

Second World War the patronage of army personnel had kept the ferryboat in business; with the end of the war against Germany in May 1945 the ferry would not have survived for long. The closure of Wawne Ferry was ultimately the decision of Moors' and Robson's Brewery (since they would have been responsible for the upkeep or replacement of the boat). As the purchasers of the Windham Arms and the ferry rights the brewery must have been aware of the likely return on their investment. Brian Newlove has suggested that Moors' and Robson's Brewery were "only interested in the drinks licence", not the ferry or the farm. The fact that Harold Walker had auctioned off all the livestock and equipment from Ferry Farm before he left would support this view. Walter Twidale was the nephew of Donald Brewer and the cousin of Harold Walker and was probably aware of how little money the ferry was generating by August 1946. He may have considered that the effort involved in running a ferry service for little reward was not worth the trouble. Furthermore, with wage levels rising at this time, it is unlikely that either Walter Twidale or Moors' and Robson's would have been willing to provide a substitute ferryman.

Ronald Dixon's lack of success with Moors' and Robson's Brewey did not deter him, even though he admitted that there was "no known law to force a ferry service". (73) As a member of Beverley Rural District Council he tried to persuade them (in December 1946) that Wawne Ferry was a public ferry and that the RDC should write to East Yorkshire County Council about the matter. (74) His moves were opposed by the RDC's chairman, Councillor H. Makrill who reported that he had spoken to the Clerk of the County Council about the ferry some months previously. Makrill told the RDC that as a result of this conversation he believed that Wawne Ferry was a private ferry rather than a public one and that, in any case, the Rural District Council had no jurisdiction in the matter. Makrill's opinion was that the issue of Wawne Ferry "was one for the Ministry of Transport." Ronald Dixon pleaded in vain for "some action to be taken" as he was convinced that it was a public ferry but Makrill's arguments won the day. The RDC voted by 17 to 1 that the Rural District Council "should not take up the matter with the County Council." (75)

Despite these setbacks Ronald Dixon continued to insist that Wawne Ferry was a public ferry and therefore it "could not be closed at the will of the man who owned the boat." (76) Taking their lead from him Woodmansey Parish Council agreed that since the closure of the ferry "was a serious matter for the residents of Wawne they would support Wawne Parish Council in any action they proposed to take."

By March 1947 the County Council too was involved because of complaints about "the inconvenience caused" by the closure of the ferry. (77) The Clerk of the County Council wrote to Wawne Parish Council asking for "information on the regular use of Wawne Ferry when in operation." (78) East Yorkshire County Council had, in fact, been investigating the ferry as early as January 1943 while making clear, at every opportunity, that they did not consider themselves responsible for it. The Council, as the relevant highway authority, was contacted by the Ministry of Transport to enquire if they might be willing to enter into an agreement with Moors and Robson's Brewery to restore the ferry service. The response of the County Council to this suggestion was predictably unenthusiastic while Moors and Robson's remained adamant that "no obligation rested on them or their tenant to maintain the ferry" (79)

Under the Ferries Act of 1919 local authorities in England and Wales had been given the power to purchase or accept transfer of a ferry and improve it. However, it seems that the tactic of East Yorkshire County Council was to persuade others, notably Moors' and Robson's Brewery, to take responsibility. The reluctance of East Yorkshire County Council to buy Wawne Ferry is not surprising given the considerable expense of running a ferry service for little reward.

The Stixwould Ferry, over the River Witham in Lincolnshire, had been purchased by Kesteven Council in 1937 (under the Ferries Act of 1919). It was a decision they were soon to regret because within ten years of buying it changes in traffic conditions meant that virtually no vehicles were using the ferry. From January 1945 Kesteven Council were paying a local woman two pounds ten shillings a week to operate the Stixwould Ferry and allowing her to keep the tolls estimated at seven shillings a week. In a fact-finding tour of ferries in Great Britain members of the Ferries Committee visited the Stixwould Ferry and spoke to councillors who believed that they were under a legal obligation to continue the ferry service and might suffer court action if they closed it. At this meeting it was stated that "the Council would like to be relieved of the liability but they could not abandon the ferry without laying themselves open to an action by some person suffering damage on that account." The County Surveyor of Kesteven Council told the investigators that the ferry carried no traffic of any consequence: only eight passengers and one vehicle per day used it and that a new pontoon would cost four hundred pounds if the old one ever needed replacement. (80)

During March 1947 the Assistant Registrar of Deeds for the East Riding, Fred Milner, was hard at work investigating the past ownership of Wawne Ferry with the intention of discovering where responsibility for it rested. He was unable to prove through a study of the documents that any public rights had been infringed and seems to have suggested, initially, that it was a private ferry. Speculating a little he said: "the public have paid a fee to use it and as it is possible that the income is insufficient to maintain the boat and pay the wages of the person operating the ferry." (81)

With pressure on the County Council mounting, Fred Milner, assisted by a Mr Mainprize who complied a brief history of ownership, did further research. In October 1947, Milner concluded "as the ferry seems to have belonged to

Wawne for more than 800 years, the obligation to maintain the ferry rests with the present owners." His argument now was that Wawne Ferry was a franchise ferry by prescription with rights and obligations confirmed by royal grant. Legally, a ferry was considered to be part of the highway and ferry owners, in return for a monopoly, "had a duty which may be enforced in the courts to carry all wayfarers across the river." (82) If the County Council had been able to prove that Wawne Ferry was a franchise ferry then, it was argued, the only way the ferry could have been legally closed was by an act of Parliament. Milner suggested, in October 1947, that the issue of the ferry had become confused with the issue of ownership of the Windham Arms and its thirty-three acre farm and that "a ferry is wholly unconnected with the ownership or occupation of land and that a ferry owner is bound to maintain safe and suitable boats ready for the use of the public and to employ fit persons as ferrymen." (83)

The same kind of legal problem was in evidence at the Horning-Woodbastwick Ferry which operated across the River Bure in Norfolk. Here the chain ferry service had ended when enemy action had rendered the pontoon unserviceable. Only a small boat then remained to ferry pedestrians and cyclists. In 1947 this ferry was investigated by the Ferries Committee of the Department of Transport who said that although " this ferry is thought to be an ancient franchise ferry and to have existed from time immemorial, there appears to be some doubt as to the legal position and the liability of the owners to provide a public ferry service." (84) Despite the fact that only three or four vehicles per week had used the Woodbastwick pontoon in the late thirties, the Ferries Committee recommended that the service should be restored. (85)

Following the advice of Fred Milner, in early January 1948 the Highways and Bridges Committee of East Riding County Council again discussed the issue of Wawne Ferry. Milner's research indicated, it was said, "the presumption of the existence of a franchise imposing an obligation upon the ferry owners." The outcome of the meeting was a letter to Moors' and Robson's Breweries Ltd in which they were informed that since the Council considered Wawne Ferry to be a franchise ferry "the ferry service should be resumed at an early date." (86) It seems the Council's view was ignored. Since the ferry was no longer financially viable Moor's and Robsons' Brewery, supported by the legal opinions of their solicitors Laverack, Son and Wray of Parliament Street Hull, were steadfast in maintaining that Wawne Ferry was a private ferry rather than a public one.

Despite the protests the ferry remained closed. In his book, Rambles around Hull, Thomas Stainforth describes a route from Wawne to Meaux and Routh and says " we can commence at Wawne which can be reached either from Sutton or the Beverley High Road by way of Thearne and Wawne Ferry". However, in a footnote to this statement he said "at the time of going to press (March 1948), the ferryboat service is suspended." (87) Although this might imply that the closure was temporary, in fact it was permanent. In 1950 the Twidales left the Windham Arms and from the 12th December 1950 a new tenant was appointed called Sydney Preston. His tenancy agreement with Moors' and Robson's Brewery specified that he should pay £30 per year for the Windham Arms and "refrain from using the above named premises for agriculture." (88) Although Moors' and Robson's still owned the ferry rights, there was no suggestion in Preston's tenancy agreement that he should run a ferry. Sydney Preston was a road transport operator from Hull whose business had became part of the nationalised British Road Services. (89) Alf Mann, newly released from National Service in 1950 did casual farm work for him at 2s 0d an hour and states categorically that Preston did not operate any kind of ferry service for pub customers or otherwise and that there was no boat. His assertion is supported by the writings of John Wilson Smith who visited the Windham Arms in 1952 and said: "the landing stage of the ferry is derelict and deeply covered in mud." (90)

When Preston took over it was reported that the Windham Arms was in a terrible state of repair and desolation but that considerable renovation had taken place in 1951. Sydney Preston continued to run the Windham Arms until 26th September 1962 when Richard Nicholson took over the tenancy at £60 per year. (91) Richard Nicholson was the final tenant with the Windham Arms itself closing as a public house in March 1967. (92) Like Sydney Preston before him, Richard Nicholson was not asked to run any kind of ferry service although he did own a rowing boat and occasionally, as a favour, ferried friends across the river to the Windham Arms. However, since this was merely a private arrangement and was done without charge it can hardly be regarded as a resurrection of the public ferry. The Nicholsons also discovered the remains of the pontoon lying on the riverbed although when they tried to bring it to the surface using a tractor the chain which had hauled the pontoon from bank to bank broke. (93)

Image above: The Windham Arms around 1952 with the pontoon ferry at the edge of the river derelict and abandoned.

Image above: The Windham Arms at Wawne in the early 1950s

The closure of the Windham Arms in March 1967 meant that the final link with Wawne Ferry was broken to. Like many other river ferries which closed in the late 1940's residents of Wawne, Thearne and elsewhere resented the loss of a service to which they had become accustomed, even if they had used it rarely. Ronald Dixon and others complained about the long distances which school children had to travel in order to cross the river (94) although it seems that this was more of an inconvenience than a real problem since the County Council did make alternative travel arrangements for Wawne scholarship children attending Beverley schools. (95) Ronald Dixon seems to have been a little annoyed that the campaign to re-open the ferry was limited to Woodmansey and that "Wawne Parish Council were not taking any action although it affected them more than the people this side of the river." (96)

With memories of the ferry service still recent local residents continued to complain about the closure into the 1950's and agitated for "a bridge or at any rate for a resumption of the ferry." (97) Public complaints about the loss of ferry services were a normal response in other parts of the country too as the Ferries Committee discovered during their investigations of 1947. Thus, in their report into the Horning-Woodbastwick Ferry (Norfolk) they commented on the "representations from local residents for the restoration of the facilities which were formerly available." (98) However, despite the complaints it is apparent that Wawne Ferry and others like it were no longer relevant in age of motor transport especially when this coincided with the appearance of more bridges. River ferries, like that at Wawne, provided transport for a gentler age of horse-drawn vehicles, cycles and pedestrians when time mattered less. The Ferries Committee of 1947-48 did not investigate Wawne Ferry since both the pontoon and the punt had ceased operating by the end of 1946. However their report is as relevant to Wawne as it is to other places when they commented that some ferries "have long since outlived their usefulness." (99)

Postscript:

Almost seventy years have now elapsed since the closure of Wawne Ferry. In that time the area has been transformed by the continuing growth of Hull with new housing estates, like Bransholme, swallowing up the farmland that once separated Wawne from Sutton-on-Hull. Arguments about the closure of Wawne Ferry or the building of a bridge to replace it have now been rendered superfluous by the construction of the Ennerdale Bridges serving to open up Hull's newest suburb Kingswood. Downstream from Wawne they comprise a pair of single leaf bascule spans, one for each carriageway, and opened in 1997.

Image above: The site of Wawne Ferry in 2003

Footnotes:

1 River Ferries, Nancy Martin,,p.ix
2 Sutton Bransholme and Wawne, Merril Rhodes, p 121
3 VCH, Vol I, p387
4 VCH, Vol I, p.389
5 VCH, Vol VI, p.169
6 T. Codrington, Roman Roads in Britain
7 VCH, Vol VII, p.184
8 ERCA, DDBD 89/4, Report to the proprietors of the low grounds and carrs affected by the Beverley and Barmston Drainage (1852), p.34
9 ERCA, DDX 328 /11
10 History of Hull, Hugh Calvert,p.19
11 ERCA, DDX/ 328/ 11
12 RAC Guide and Handbook 1927-8, p342
13 ERCA, DDX 328/11
14 VCH, Vol VI, p.297
15 VCH, Vol VI , p271
16 G. Poulson , History and Antiquities of the Seignory of Holderness, vol 2, p281, p293
17 Edward Bond (editor): The Chronicles of Melsa, Volume One, page xxv and page 171
18 Rhodes, p6
19 A Brief History of Beverley, T. Lambert, p1
20 An Historical Atlas of East Yorkshire, p40
21 Calvert, p15
22 ERCA, DDX 328/11
23 Domesday Book,2E 18B
24 ERCA, DDX/1759/1/76
25 The Lords of Holderness, B. English,p.201
26 Sutton, Bransholme and Wawne, M. Rhodes p.3
27 inf. From Mrs A. Los
28 Inf. From Brian Newlove
29 VCH Vol 6 /British history online p.295-301
30 VCH, vol1, p.473

31 Calvert, p.19
32 VCH, vol1, p473
33 Bulmers Directory, 1892
34 ERCA, DDX/328/11
35 Lambert, p2
36 Lambert p. 3
37 VCH, vol. VII, p.184
38 ERCA, DDX/328/11
39 M. Carrick, Lords of the Manor of Wawne, E.Y.L.S bulletin vol 1
40 Rhodes, p27
41 A History of Hull, E. Gillett and K. MacMahon, p.172
42 History of the Town and County of Kingston-upon-Hull, J. Tickell, p.463
43 G. Oliver, History of Beverley, p. 222
44 ERCA, DSF/38/B/4
45 ERCA DSF/113/B/1
46 ERCA, DDER 42/17
47 ERCA, DSF 1235/ D/ 3
48 K.A. MacMahon, Roads and Turnpike Trusts in East Yorkshire
49 ERCA, DDER 42/22
50 ERCA, Wawne Account Book, DDIV 21/3, June 26th 1776
51 ERCA DSF/ 277/C/5
52 Wawne Account Book, Jan 4th 1783: Charges of a dinner when Mr Clough and Mr Judson were "taking possession of Wawne Passage House at Wawne, £1   12s   0d"
53 inf. from East Riding of Yorkshire Council Conservation and Enforcement Unit
54 Holderness in Picture and Story vol.6, The Country Inns, J. Wilson Smith, p.305
55 ERCA, Wawne Account Book, July 31st and August 3rd 1779, September 20th 1780
56 ERCA. Wawne Account Book, August 25th 1781
57 Wawne Account Book, November 10th 1778 and April 11th 1779
58 Wawne Account Book, 1794 Hull Directory and 1780 Hull

Poll Book
59 Wawne Account Book, January 26th 1780
60 Carrick, p44
61 Wawne Account Book, July 22nd 1780
62 Wawne Account Book, November 24th 1780
63 Baines's Directory, 1823, Wawne, professions and trades
64 ERCA, List of Licenses Granted, ODT/2/7/224
65 1851 Census
66 Beverley Guardian, December 13th 1862
67 Information from Penny Stewart
68 1881 Census
69 Information from Penny Stewart
70 1901 Census
71 ERCA, DCBB/5/21: Letter of Joseph Tiffin to Charles Simons (contractor)
72 ERCA, DCBB/5/21, Letter from Edward Knox to Henry Bainton, 15th October 1885
73 ERCA DCBB, Letter from Edward Knox to Henry Bainton, 17th October 1885
74 The Old Grovehill Ferry Bridge, K.Crosby, p1-5
75 York Herald, June 9th 1899
76 Hull Daily Mail, June 8th 1899
77 Beverley Guardian, 10th June 1899
78 Hull Daily Mail, June 8th 1899
79 The East Riding Telegraph, June 1st 1895
80 The East Riding Telegraph, June 15th 1895
81 1901 Census
82 Jack Clarkson Remembers, Chapter 1 : The Wawne Ferry, p2
83 York Herald, May 12th 1888
84 Eastern Morning News, April 17th 1888
85 Eastern Morning News, April 18th 1888
86 Eastern Morning News, April 19th 1888
87 Report of the Ferries Committee, 1948, p7
88 Jack Clarkson Remembers, p2
89 Report of the Ferries Committee, 1948, p8
90 Inf. From Mr C.Nicklas, Beverley
91 PRO, MT10/1868, H776/1916

92 ERCA, DDX 328/11
93 Beverley Guardian, January 7th 1888
94 Burke's Landed Gentry, vol 2, p.650
95 Rhodes, p.113
96 ibid
97 HCCA, DBHT/9/768
98 ibid
99 Bulmer's Directory, 1892
100 Woodmansey Parish Council Minutes, 18th December 1946
101 Lost Houses of East Yorkshire, David Neave and Edward Waterson, p60

Footnotes for Chapter Three and Chapter Four
1 Ferries Committee Report, 1948
2 Minutes of the East Riding County Council Highways and Bridges Committee, 4th July 1938
3 Jack Clarkson Remembers, p3
4 Jack Clarkson, p3
5 G.B. Wood , Ferries and Ferrymen, p15
6 Yorkshire Evening Post, January 14th 1922
7 Hull Daily Mail, April 6th 1936
8 Hull Daily Mail, September 17th 1938
9 Hull Daily Mail, 31st August 1907
10   Hull Daily Mail, Jan 21st 1938
11 East Yorkshire Motor Services 1926-1983, Ian Gibbs
12 Inf. From J. Beaulah
13 Inf. From Mrs A. Hinch
14 Inf. From Mr J. Robinson
15 Hull Daily Mail, March 13th 1922
16 Inf. From Mr L. Heathcote / Mrs A. Hinch
17   Hull Daily Mail, October 18th 1944
18   Hull Daily Mail, May 25th 1922
19   Hull Daily Mail, May 9th 1934
20   Rhodes, p118-119
21 Inf. Mrs J. Davies
22   Rhodes, p.118
23 Inf. From Mrs Cawood

24 Inf. From Mrs A. Hinch
25 Inf. From Mr C. Nicklas
26 Jack Clarkson Remembers, p3
27 York Herald, December 6th 1895
28 North Eastern Daily Gazette, December 6th 1895
29 W. Fawcett, The Holderness Hunt, p28
30 Bulmers Guide: Parish Information (1892)
31 Hunting Notes From Holderness, F. Reynard, p.241
32 Jack Clarkson Remembers, p3
33 Inf. From Mr J. Beaulah
34 inf. From :Mr L. Heathcote/ Mrs J. Gibbins
35 inf. From Mr J. Lawson / Mr J. Beaulah
36 inf. From Mr A. Mann/ Mr L. Heathcote
37 Inf from Annie Hinch / Hull Daily Mail, May 4th 1939
38 VCH, Vol VII, p.185
39 Inf. From A. Mann
40 Inf. From F. Norton
41 Inf from Brian Newlove
42 Hull Daily Mail, May 27th 1898
43 ERCA, Highways and Bridges Committee Minute Book, 11th April,1919
44 Hull Daily Mail: Our Holderness Letter, March 26th 1921
45 ERCA, Highways and Bridges Committee Minute Book, 1st October 1945
46 inf. From Video on Woodmansey, Dunswell and Thearne (section on Wawne Ferry)
47 ERCA: CD1, 24th March 1941
48 ERCA, CD31, Enemy Air Activity in the East Riding, Thurs 17th July 1941
49 Eastern Morning News, July 6th 1886, VCH East Riding Vol 1, p390
50 VCH, Vol. 1, p.470
51 Hull Daily Mail, July 8th 1937
52 Inf. From Mike Jackson
53 Inf from Brian Newlove 54 The eight were: the Horning-Woodbastwick (River Bure, Norfolk)), BuckenhamClaxton (River Yare, Norfolk), Surlingham-Postwick (River

Yare,Norfolk), Southwold-Walberswick (River Blyth, Suffolk), Bawdsey-Felixstowe (River Deben,Suffolk) Bredon-Twyning (Worcestershire,River Severn), Pixham (Worcestershire,River Severn), Eccleston (Cheshire,River Dee)
55 Nancy Martin, River Ferries, p50
56 PRO, MT41/53 5
57 PRO, MT41/49
58　Inf. From Brian Newlove
59 Inf. From Mr A. Mann
60 ERCA, DDX 328/11, Inf. From Mrs A. Hinch/ Mr C. Nicklas
61 Inf. From Mr A. Mann
62 Moors and Robsons Minute Books, p151-152
63　Hull Daily Mail, 9th August 1946
64 Inf. From M. Botham
65 1947 Electoral Register
66　1911 Census
67　Inf from the 1911 Census and Penny Stewart
68 VCH, Vol VI, p.297
69　Inf. from Penny Stewart
70　Hull Daily Mail, December 27th 1927
71　Woodmansey Parish Council Minutes, 18th December 1946, p.201-202, Beverley Guardian: March 8th 1947,p.1
72 River Ferries, Nancy Martin, p.49
73 Woodmansey Parish Council Minutes, 18th December 1946
74 Beverley Rural District Council Minutes, 19th December 1946
75　Beverley Rural District Council (Minutes of the Council in Committee, Jan 2nd 1947)
76　Beverley Guardian, 8th March 1947, p1
77 ERCA, DDX/328/11
78 Wawne Parish Council Minutes, 28th March 1947
79 East Riding County Council Minutes, 31st March 1947
80 PRO, MT 41/ 50
81　ERCA: DDX 328/11 (correspondence of Fred Milner to Miss Rodmell)
82 Nancy Martin, River Ferries, p1

83 ERCA, DDX 328/11
84 PRO, MT41/51
85 Report of the Ferries Committee (1948), p14-15
86 ERCA, Highways and Bridges Committee Minutes, 5th January 1948
87 T. Stainforth, Rambles Around Hull, p.25
88 Moors and Robson's Minute Book, p301
89 Inf.From Mr A. Mann / Mr J. Lawson
90 J. Wilson Smith, Holderness in Picture and Story: Vol 6, the Country Inns, p. 305
91 Moors and Robson Minute Book, p.234
92 inf. From Richard Nicholson
93 inf. From John Nicholson
94 Beverley Rural District Council Minutes, December 19th 1946
95 Beverley Rural District Council Minutes, January 2nd 1947
96 Woodmansey Parish Council Minutes, 26th February 1947, p.206
97 J. Wilson Smith, Holderness in Picture and Story, vol 6, p.303
98 Report of the Ferries Committee, 1948, p15
99 Report of the Ferries Committee, 1948, p7

Printed in Great Britain
by Amazon